For Mom & Dad, grazers extraordinaire.

Grazing

Portable snacks and finger foods

for anytime, anywhere.

Julie Van Rosendaal

Notice

This book is intended as a reference only, not to replace medical advice. Nutritional needs vary from person to person; the foods discussed and the recipes given here are designed to help you make informed choices about your diet and health.

Published by One Smart Cookie Inc.
P.O. Box 32044
2619 – 14 Street SW
Calgary, Alberta T2T 5X6
(800) 870-1265

www.onesmartcookie.ca

Printed in Canada

Book design, layout and production:
John Vickers, Julie Van Rosendaal,
Meg Van Rosendaal, Mike Semenchuk

Photography & food styling:
Julie Van Rosendaal, Mike Semenchuk,
Meg Van Rosendaal

Editing: Alison Boyd, Meg Van Rosendaal

Library and Archives
Canada Cataloguing in Publication

Van Rosendaal, Julie, 1970-
Grazing : portable snacks and finger foods for anytime, anywhere / Julie Van Rosendaal.

Includes index.
ISBN 0-9687563-1-X

1. Snack foods. 2. Appetizers. I. Title.

TX740.V35 2005 641.8'12   C2004-906040-6

Nutritional analyses have been calculated using the Food Smart Business Edition program. When a choice is given, analysis is based on the first listed ingredient. Optional ingredients are not included. When milk is called for, 1% milk is used in the analysis.

Cover Photos (clockwise from top left)
Olive & Garlic Breadsticks with Romesco Dip, Vietnamese Rice Paper Rolls with Peanut Dip, Chocolate Swirl Banana Bread and Peppermint Patties, Goong Waan (Sweet & Spicy Shrimp), Spicy Cheese Fries, Spanakopita (Spinach & Feta) Triangles, Maple Pecan Popcorn.

Contents

Garlic Roasted Potato Skins 41

Pita Chips 42
- Curried Pita Chips

Bagel Chips 43
- Olive Oil & Garlic Bagel Chips

Crostini 43

Wonton Crisps 44
- Sesame, Garlic & Parmesan Wonton Crisps
- Cinnamon Sugar Wonton Crisps
- Spicy Curry Wonton Crisps
- Salt and Pepper Wonton Crisps

Flour Tortillas 45
- Mini Flour Tortillas

Cinnamon Sugar Tortilla Chips 46
- Baked Tortilla Chips

Chili Lime Corn Chips 47

Parmesan Toasts 47

Quick Breadsticks 48
- Pesto Breadsticks
- Olive & Garlic Breadsticks

Rosemary Parmesan Twists 49

Dip, Spread, Dunk & Smear 51

Spinach & Artichoke Dip 52
- Crab, Spinach & Artichoke Dip
- Caesar or Salsa Spinich & Artichoke Dip

Hot Crab & Artichoke Dip 53

Caramelized Onion Dip 54
- Caramelized Onion & Spinach Dip
- Warm Chevre Dip

Chili con Queso Dip 55
- Spinach Con Queso Dip
- Bean Con Queso Dip

Seven Layer Dip 56

Cheesy Black Bean Dip 57
- Black Bean & Bacon Dip

Chorizo Chipotle Dip 58

Creamy Chicken & Charred Corn Dip 59

Guacamole 60

- Guacamole with Pears, Grapes & Pomegranate

Edamamole 61

Classic Tomato Salsa 62
- Avocado Salsa

Olive & Basil Salsa 63

Black Bean & Mango Salsa 63

Pico de Gallo 64

Curried Shrimp Chutney Dip 65

Hummus 66
- Roasted Red Pepper Hummus
- Mediterranean Hummus
- Spicy Hummus
- Balsamic Onion Hummus
- Pumpkin Hummus
- Roasted Garlic Hummus
- Roasted Garlic Edamame Hummus
- Roasted Carrot Hummus
- Fresh Pea Hummus

Roasted Garlic & White Bean Spread 68
- Baked White Bean Spread
- White Bean & Roasted Red Pepper Spread
- Italian White Bean Spread
- Yogurt & Feta White Bean Spread
- White Bean Guacamole

Tzatziki 70

Artichoke Tzatziki Dip 70

Baba Ghanouj 71
- Creamy Baba Ghanouj
- Roasted Eggplant & Tomato Dip

Roasted Red Pepper & Garlic Dip 72

Roasted Red Pepper & Feta Dip 73
- Feta Chili Dip

Olive Tapenade 74
- Olive & Sun-dried Tomato Tapenade
- Mushroom Tapenade

Antipasto 75

Radish & Roasted Red Pepper Dip 76

Buttermilk Peppercorn Dip 77

Curried Veggie Dip 77

Romesco Dip 78

Muhammara 79

Fruit Dips 80
- Creamy Fruit Dip
- Strawberry Fruit Dip
- Sour Cream with Brown Sugar
- Marshmallow Peach Fruit Dip
- Dulce de Leche
- Creamy Key Lime Dip
- Chocolate Fondue

Cranberry Orange Goat Cheese Schmear 81
Creamy & Spicy Tuna Schmear 81

Finger Lickin' Food 83

Chicken Fingers with Honey Mustard 84
- Curried Almond Chicken Fingers
- Pecan Crusted Chicken Fingers
- Spicy Chicken Fingers
- Crunchy Buffalo Chicken Fingers
- Crispy Sesame Chicken Fingers

Buffalo Drumsticks 86
Sticky, Spicy Drumsticks 87
Cheese Sticks 88
Mini 'Toad-in-the-Hole' 89
- Mini Yorkshire Puddings
  with Roast Beef & Horseradish Cream

Goong Waan (Sweet & Spicy Shrimp) 90
Curried Peanut Shrimp 91
Basic Pizza Crust 92
- Flavored Pizza Dough

BBQ Chicken Pizza 93
Caramelized Onion, Feta & Olive Pizza 94
Potato Skins 95
Green Eggs with Ham 96
Smoked Salmon Devilled Eggs 97
Balsamic Mushroom Crostini 98
- Balsamic Mushroom Dip

Roasted Pearl Onion Crostini 99
- Roasted Pearl Onion Crostini with Cambozola

Bruschetta 100
- Smashed Cherry Tomato & Olive Bruschetta

White Bean, Tomato & Olive Bruschetta
  with Goat Cheese 101
Tomato, Avocado & Shrimp Bruschetta 102
Chicken, Black Bean
  & Mushroom Quesadilla 102
Quesadilla Variations 103
California Rolls
  (Sushi with Avocado and Crab) 104

Food on a Stick 107

Chicken Satay with Peanut Sauce 108
Peanut Sauce 109
Pork Satay 110
Tandoori Chicken Satay 111
Jerk Chicken Skewers 112
BBQ Buffalo Chicken Strips
  with Blue Cheese Dip 113
Greek Lamb Kebabs 114
- Yogurt Mint Sauce
- Greek Meatballs

Teriyaki Beef Sticks 115
Honey, Ginger & Sesame Salmon Sticks 116
- Honey-Mustard Salmon Sticks
- Honey, Garlic & Ginger Sesame Chicken Sticks

Vietnamese Pork Meatballs 117
Cocktail Meatballs 118
Meatball Variations 119
- Cocktail Sausages
- Spicy Jelly Meatballs
- Sweet Hoisin Meatballs
- Sloppy Joe Meatballs

Good Things in Small Packages 121

Curried Coconut Mango Chicken
  in Wonton Cups 122
Samosas 123
- Spinach & Potato Samosas

Lovin' from the Oven 141

- Onion & Garlic Bagels
- Cheese Bagels

Onion Bialys 169

Focaccia 170

- Caramelized Onion & Parmesan Focaccia
- Olive & Feta Focaccia
- Grape Focaccia

Sweet Eats 173

Stone Fruit Tarts 174

Puffed Wheat Squares 175

Chocolate Fudge 176

Sponge Toffee 177

Chocolate Nut Brittle 178

My Grandma's Peanut Brittle 179

- Hazelnut or Almond Brittle

Quickies 181

Breadsticks 182

Crostini with Olive Tapenade 182

Mediterranean Mini Pitas 182

Turkey & Black Bean Tortilla Rolls 182

Smoked Salmon Crostini 182

Fruit, Nut & Cheese Truffles 182

Sticky Drumsticks 182

Mini California Pizzas 182

Phyllo Pizza 182

Roasted Red Pepper Quesadillas 182

Refried Bean Quesadillas 183

Sticky Peach Chicken Sticks 183

Shrimp with Orange-Chili Hoisin Sauce 183

Sun-dried Tomato, Pesto, Shrimp and Feta Pizza 183

Quick Seafood Dip 183

Quick pizza topping ideas 183

Chutney Gingersnaps 183

Crunchy Ravioli on a Stick 183

Jezebel 183

Plum Glazed Chicken 184

Stuffed Mushrooms 184

Stuffed Pretzel Nuggets 184

Peach-Cambozola Bundles 184

Thai Chicken Rolls 184

Curried Shrimp Salad Cups 184

Sticky Balsamic Prosciutto-Wrapped Dates 184

Pizza Rolls 184

Easy Chicken or Beef Satay 184

Strawberry Cheesecake Bites 185

Salami Chips 185

Peanut Butter Popcorn Balls 185

Stuffed Apricots 185

Real Fruit Gummies 185

Chili Cheese Fries 185

Tortilla Cups 185

Granola Bites 185

Olive Devilled Eggs 185

Spicy Garlic Nuts 185

Quick Veggie Dip 186

Tofu Peanut Dip 186

Prosciutto Prawns 186

Roasted Feta with Red Peppers and Olives 186

Honey Roasted Onion & Garlic Dip 186

Creamy Avocado Ranch Dip 186

Easy Bean Dip 186

Chutney Cream Cheese Schmear 186

Caramel Apples 186

Mexican Wonton Packets 186

Real Fruit Leather 187

Ginger Molasses Ice Cream Sandwiches 187

Mud Pie Ice Cream Sandwiches 187

Lettuce Wraps with Figs,
     Roasted Red Peppers and Parmesan 187

Smoothies 187

Olive & Feta Salsa 187

Chocolate Panini 187

Roasted Pumpkin Seeds 187

I like to eat. A lot.

I'm not the only one – food has always been culturally significant and eating an important social event, but in recent years it has become one of our favorite pastimes. We love to eat at home, at work, in the car, on the couch, at the movies, at school, and at every conceivable social gathering. All holidays revolve around food, and it's rare to be out of sight of a vending machine, coffee shop, convenience store or drive-thru. It's no wonder 63% of us are overweight!

Our crazy schedules and love for food makes snacking common and portable food hugely popular, whether we eat three meals a day like our Moms taught us to or not. Many of us grab whatever might pass for breakfast on the way out the door. If you eat lunch anywhere but at home you're either taking it with you or buying it somewhere. And who doesn't eat in the car?

Everyone needs a little smackerel of something after work or school or before a workout. If you have kids, they require an almost constant supply of snacks. Then there are parties and social functions, that empty space beside your latte and the absolute need to munch during a movie. Grazing has become our eating pattern of choice, and the good news is – doctors and nutritionists all over the world believe that it's the healthiest way to eat!

Eating several smaller meals and snacks over the course of the day (rather than two or three big ones) keeps your energy levels high and blood sugar levels on an even keel. Grazing also lowers your cholesterol, and consequently your risk of heart disease and stroke.

Eating regularly also keeps your mind alert and hunger at bay, which will make you less likely to become ravenous and devour enough food to sustain an entire Boy Scout troop. (Not that I'd know from personal experience or anything.)

When you're hungry, you naturally crave energy-dense (read: high calorie) foods, namely fat, which has more than double the calories of protein or carbs. When fat is combined with sugar or salt it sure tastes good. And when fatty, sugary, salty snacks are so readily available, so cheap, so highly marketed and so yummy, they're nearly impossible to resist. It's no wonder our best intentions crumble in the face of Whoppers, Krispy Kremes and Ben & Jerry's! It's important that we make good grazing choices.

Studies have shown that people who skip meals or go for long periods without eating don't perform well, and that eating too little causes your metabolism to drop and your body to hold on to energy stores in response to the famine. Conversely, big, heavy meals tend to slow us down – picture yourself lounging on the couch with your pants undone after a big turkey dinner. Our digestive system is similar to that of chimpanzees and gorillas, who nibble all day long and never overload on calories. (They also never outgrow their pants.) And eating more frequently throughout the day is natural for most kids, who have small stomachs but high energy requirements so they need a steady fuel supply.

There's nothing better than sitting down to a good meal with family and friends, but the traditional three-square-meals-a-day schedule often encourages people to eat when they think they should, rather than when they're hungry. (Whenever my cousin asks her husband if he's hungry his reply is, "I don't know, what time is it?" He eats his meals at 8, 12 and 6.) The recipes in this book can make balanced meals or just fill the gap any time of day, and are perfect for sharing, which after all, is the best part.

Now that our schedules are more hectic and mealtimes less rigid, our changing eating patterns make us lucrative targets for the snack, convenience and fast food industry, which spends billions of dollars annually to convince us we're busy (true) and don't have time to cook (not entirely true), so they can make life easier and less stressful for us (at what cost?). Snack foods, fast foods and convenience foods have the highest calorie content, the least nutritional value and the most ingredients with names you can't even pronounce, let alone categorize into a food group.

Because these kinds of products are so heavily marketed to kids, their health is suffering as well. It doesn't help when ad agencies pair junk food and pop with rock stars, Disney and Hanna-Barbera to make them even more appealing to children. Guilt is a big selling tool for grownups: if you buy Hamburger Helper or go to

McDonald's, you'll have more time to spend with your kids. (What better way to spend time together than cooking up something delicious?)

Consider the cost of convenience: when we choose fast food over healthy food (which can be just as fast), we prioritize convenience over health and money. The fact that opening a box or ordering takeout is a no-brainer also plays a role when we're stressed out, tired, and don't have any fast and easy solutions. If we're willing to spend over $50 billion a year in an attempt to solve our weight issues, shouldn't we be willing to spend a little time? What is our well-being worth, and that of our families?

If you're a grazer, a party-thrower or occasional snacker, this book is full of easy-to-prepare, portable, good-for-you and (most importantly) delicious food that doesn't require a knife and fork. It provides ammo against the vending machine, comforts you when you need to relax, and feeds a crowd when your friends are over. This is real food you can take with you wherever you go, even if it's only as far away as the couch. And most of the recipes take less time than ordering a pizza. Eat up!

Got the Munchies?

One of the secrets of successful snacking is to keep hunger at bay by giving in to the munchies. We all get the munchies – during that mid afternoon lull or in the evening in front of the TV. Most packaged foods that are intended to satisfy the munchies are a nutritional nightmare – they don't do much for you besides taste good, so it's best not to keep them in the house if you're like me and don't trust your self control in their presence. Make sure your cupboard is loaded with healthy snacks or be prepared to stir up one of these fast recipes, and when you get the munchies you'll be doing your body a favor.

Just live by Miss Piggy's motto:
Never eat more than you can lift.

Regular or Sweet Potato Oven Fries

Brightly-colored sweet potatoes are among the most nutritious of all vegetables. Besides being much higher in fiber than regular potatoes, they are very high in beta-carotene, contain the carotenoids lutein and zeaxanthin, and supply substantial amounts of vitamins C, B6 and manganese. They are delicious roasted with garlic, oil and chopped fresh rosemary.

3 medium russet or Yukon gold potatoes, peeled or unpeeled

OR

1 large sweet potato, peeled or unpeeled

1 Tbsp canola or olive oil

1 clove crushed garlic (optional)

salt or garlic powder & pepper to taste

Contents per serving

Calories	114
Total fat	3.4 g
saturated fat	0.3 g
monounsaturated fat	2.0 g
polyunsaturated fat	1.1 g
Protein	2.5 g
Carbohydrates	18.8 g
Cholesterol	0.0 mg
Fiber	1.8 g
Calories from fat	27%

1 Preheat oven to 475 F.

2 Cut potatoes into evenly sized wedges or into 1/4" - 1/2" sticks. Place them in a large bowl and cover with hot water; soak for 10 minutes. Meanwhile, coat a heavy, rimmed baking sheet with the oil. If you want, stir a crushed clove of garlic into the oil first.

3 Drain the potatoes and thoroughly dry with paper towels or a tea towel. Place on the prepared baking sheet. Sprinkle with garlic powder, salt and pepper and toss with your fingers to coat well with the oil and seasonings, arranging them in a single layer. Make sure they aren't crowded or overlapping or they will steam instead of browning properly.

4 Cover tightly with foil and bake for 5 minutes. Remove the foil and continue to bake for about 20 minutes, turning once or twice, until golden and crisp. Serve immediately.

Serves 4.

Oven baked fries are every bit as good as the deep fried kind, and are cheap, fast and easy to boot. If you're in a hurry, skip the soaking step and the foil, and simply roast the oiled potatoes for 20 - 30 minutes,

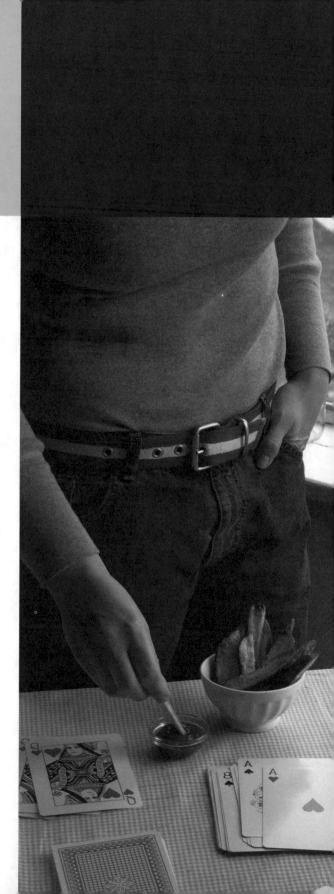

stirring once or twice. To make spicy ketchup for dipping, mix equal parts ketchup and salsa. This cuts the calorie content of ketchup, which contains more sugar than ice cream, almost in half!

Spicy Cheese Fries

Combine 1/4 cup grated Parmesan cheese, 1 tsp chili powder and 1/4 tsp each garlic powder, salt and pepper. Toss the oiled fries with the mixture before baking. These are my favorite!

Sweet & Spicy Sweet Potato Fries

Combine 1 Tbsp brown sugar, 1/2 tsp salt, a pinch of cayenne pepper and a pinch of cinnamon. Sprinkle over sweet potato fries as soon as they come out of the oven and toss (tongs work well for this) until well coated and the heat of the potatoes melts the sugar.

Baked Potato Chips

Have you ever bought those high-end, thickly sliced olive oil potato chips at a gourmet shop for $6 per bag? Last I checked, potatoes were dirt cheap! Homemade potato chips are dead easy to make, and can be seasoned however you see fit. Because they are baked with olive or canola oil, the fat you get is the healthy kind. They are of course the quintessential snack – even better when you have dip to scoop. Try the Caramelized Onion Dip (see page 54).

3 medium russet or Yukon gold potatoes, peeled or unpeeled

OR

1 large sweet potato, peeled or unpeeled

1-2 Tbsp canola, olive or walnut oil

1 clove garlic, crushed, or

1/4 tsp garlic powder (optional)

1/2 tsp each salt and pepper

Contents per serving

Calories	86
Total fat	2.4 g
saturated fat	0.3 g
monounsaturated fat	2.0 g
polyunsaturated fat	0.1 g
Protein	17.0 g
Carbohydrates	12.6 g
Cholesterol	0.0 mg
Fiber	1.2 g
Calories from fat	35%

1. Preheat oven to 450 F.

2. Scrub potatoes and slice lengthwise or widthwise into very thin, uniform slices. A mandolin does the best job.

3. If you are using garlic, stir it into the oil. Brush two baking sheets, preferably non-stick, with about 1/2 Tbsp of oil and place in the oven to heat for about 10 minutes.

4. Remove the baking sheets from the oven and arrange potato slices on sheets in a single layer. Bake until potatoes are golden on the bottom side, about 20 minutes. Turn potatoes over and bake until they are golden brown all over, about 15 - 20 minutes more.

5. Transfer to paper towels to cool. Repeat with the remaining potatoes.

Serves 4.

Kettle Corn

This is a little more caramelly than regular kettle corn, but it's the same perfect marriage of salty, sweet and crunchy. It's really fast and easy to make when you need a caramel corn fix.

1 bag light butter-flavored microwave popcorn, popped

1/2 cup sugar

2 Tbsp water

1 tsp butter

Contents per serving

Calories	200
Total fat	3.7 g
saturated fat	0.6 g
monounsaturated fat	3.0 g
polyunsaturated fat	0.0 g
Protein	2.1 g
Carbohydrates	40.7 g
Cholesterol	2.6 mg
Fiber	0.0 g
Calories from fat	16%

1. Place the popcorn in a large bowl. If you like, spray the bowl first with non-stick spray to keep it from sticking.

2. Combine sugar, water and butter in a small saucepan over medium heat. Bring to a boil, stirring constantly. Reduce heat to medium-low and simmer for 10 minutes, swirling pan occasionally but not stirring, until the sugar is deep golden. Immediately pour over the popcorn and quickly stir to coat. Tongs work great for this!

3. Cool and eat. (It's usually cool enough for me by the time I get from the kitchen to the living room.)

Serves 4.

Chocolate Popcorn
Once the sugar is deep golden, quickly stir in 2 Tbsp cocoa and pour over the popcorn, tossing to coat.

Banana Split Popcorn Mix
Add 1 cup banana chips, 1/2 cup dried cherries, 1/2 cup peanuts and 1/4 cup chocolate chips to the cooled popcorn.

Maple Pecan Popcorn

This is one of those snacks that I can't have at arm's reach or I'll likely polish off half the bowl. It's also one of those recipes that will win you a lot of friends. Some Christmases I buy old mason jars and fill them with maple pecan popcorn to give away as gifts. Use more inexpensive grade B maple syrup if you like.

8 cups air popped popcorn (about 1/3 cup kernels)

1 cup pure maple syrup

2 Tbsp butter

1/4 tsp salt

1/2 cup chopped pecans, toasted (optional)

Contents per serving

Calories	163
Total fat	4.0 g
saturated fat	2.5 g
monounsaturated fat	1.2 g
polyunsaturated fat	0.3 g
Protein	1.3 g
Carbohydrates	31.0 g
Cholesterol	10.4 mg
Fiber	1.6 g
Calories from fat	23%

1 Toss popcorn and pecans in a large bowl that has been sprayed with non-stick spray.

2 In a small saucepan, bring maple syrup, butter and salt to a boil. Reduce heat and continue to boil for 15 - 20 minutes, until the mixture reaches 300 F on a candy thermometer (hard crack stage). If you don't have a candy thermometer, drizzle some of the syrup into ice water and it should separate into hard brittle threads that break when bent.

3 Pour over the popcorn and quickly stir to coat completely. Spread on a baking sheet to cool.

Serves 6.

Maple Cranberry Pecan Popcorn
Add 1/4 cup dried cranberries to the popcorn-pecan mixture.

Flavored Popcorn

Here are some great spice blends to sprinkle on your popcorn. I find they won't stick to dry air popped popcorn, so I like to sprinkle them over light buttered microwave popcorn and shake it up in the bag while it's still warm. That way the popcorn tastes buttery too! If you do it this way, you may want to eliminate the salt, since microwave popcorn is already salted. The nutritional analysis will really depend on the brand of popcorn you use – the spices add virtually no calories. The Parmesan cheese adds 57 calories and 3.6 grams of fat per 2 Tbsp. You could also try using prepared powdered dip mixes, such as ranch and dill.

1 bag light microwave popcorn,
or several cups air-popped

Cajun

1 tsp salt (optional, if using plain popcorn)

1 tsp paprika

1/2 tsp each onion and garlic powder

1/4 tsp black pepper

pinch cayenne pepper (optional)

Southwestern Chili Cheese

2 Tbsp grated Parmesan cheese

1 tsp salt (optional, if using plain popcorn)

1 tsp ground cumin

1/2 tsp chili powder

Italian

2 Tbsp grated Parmesan cheese

1 tsp salt (optional, if using plain popcorn)

1/4 tsp dried oregano, basil
or Italian seasoning

Grinding fresh black pepper

Curry

1 tsp salt (optional, if using plain popcorn)

1/2 tsp curry powder

Pinch turmeric and a good grinding
of black pepper

Pesto

2 Tbsp grated Parmesan cheese

1 tsp dried basil, crushed

1/4 tsp garlic powder

Party Mix

I know, party mix is kitschy. But I bet if someone put a bowl of it in front of you, you would eat some.

3 cups air popped popcorn
or light buttery microwave popcorn

3 cups Shreddies or Chex cereal

2 cups pretzel sticks

1/2 cup roasted peanuts, salted or unsalted

2 Tbsp melted butter or olive oil

1 Tbsp soy sauce

1 Tbsp Worcestershire sauce

1 Tbsp sugar

1 tsp lemon juice

1/2 tsp curry powder (optional)

1/2 tsp garlic salt

1/4 tsp black pepper

pinch cayenne pepper

2 Tbsp grated Parmesan cheese (optional)

1. Preheat oven to 300 F.

2. In a large bowl toss together the popcorn, cereal, pretzel sticks and nuts. In a small dish stir together the butter, soy sauce, Worcestershire sauce, sugar, lemon juice, curry powder, garlic salt, pepper and cayenne. Drizzle over the cereal mixture and toss until evenly coated, then spread in a shallow roasting pan. If you like, sprinkle the lot with Parmesan cheese.

3. Bake for 45 minutes, stirring often, until toasted. Store in an airtight container.

Makes about 9 cups.

Contents per cup

Calories	200
Total fat	6.8 g
saturated fat	2.3 g
monounsaturated fat	2.9 g
polyunsaturated fat	1.6 g
Protein	5.1 g
Carbohydrates	30.7 g
Cholesterol	6.9 mg
Fiber	3.4 g
Calories from fat	31%

Caramel Corn

I am such a fan of caramel corn that I only make it when I know I'll have friends around to help me eat it! A giant bowl of caramel corn is the ultimate test of self control. Each popcorn kernel contains a tiny amount of water that, when heated, causes pressure to build until the kernel turns itself inside out. Too many unpopped kernels is a sign that your stash has dried out. To prolong its shelf life, store your kernels in an airtight container in the fridge or freezer.

8 cups air popped popcorn
(about 1/3 cup kernels)

1 cup packed brown sugar

1/2 cup corn syrup or liquid honey

2 Tbsp butter

1 tsp vanilla

1/4 tsp baking soda

1/2 cup roasted peanuts, almonds, pecans
or other nuts (optional)

Contents per cup

Calories	196
Total fat	2.6 g
saturated fat	1.6 g
monounsaturated fat	0.8 g
polyunsaturated fat	0.2 g
Protein	0.9 g
Carbohydrates	43.1 g
Cholesterol	6.9 mg
Fiber	1.1 g
Calories from fat	13%

1 Preheat oven to 250 F.

2 Spray a large bowl with non-stick spray and put the popcorn in it, along with the nuts if you're using them.

3 Combine the brown sugar, corn syrup and butter in a medium saucepan and bring to a boil over medium heat. Boil without stirring, swirling the pan occasionally, for 4 minutes. Remove from heat and stir in the vanilla and baking soda. It will foam up at first.

4 Quickly pour over the popcorn and stir to coat well. Tongs work really well for this! Spread onto a cookie sheet or roasting pan and bake for 30 minutes, stirring once or twice. Cool.

Makes about 9 cups.

Cracker Jack

For caramel corn that tastes more like Cracker Jack, use half corn syrup and half dark molasses. Add 1/2 cup roasted peanuts as well.

My Granola

Homemade granola is a virtuous thing. It's cheap (compared to the store-bought variety), insanely easy to make, low in saturated fat, and you can add any combination of fruit, nuts and seeds to suit your taste. Ground flaxseed, hulled green pumpkin seeds, sunflower seeds, pine nuts, pecans, walnuts, and sliced or slivered almonds all make great additions and add protein, fiber, vitamins and minerals. If you're a molasses fan, replace some of the honey or maple syrup with it. If you like coconut but not the saturated fat, add coconut extract instead of vanilla. Many recipes call for lots of butter or oil but I've discovered you don't need it or miss it!

6 cups old fashioned (large flake) oats

1/2 - 1 cup chopped nuts (sliced almonds, pecans, walnuts or a combination)

pinch cinnamon (optional)

1/4 tsp salt

1 cup dried fruit, such as raisins, cranberries, cherries, chopped dates, apricots, apples and pears

1/2 cup honey

1/2 cup maple syrup

1 tsp vanilla

Contents per 1/3 cup

Calories	179
Total fat	3.0 g
saturated fat	0.5 g
monounsaturated fat	1.6 g
polyunsaturated fat	0.9 g
Protein	4.4 g
Carbohydrates	34.6 g
Cholesterol	0.0 mg
Fiber	3.3 g
Calories from fat	16%

1 Preheat oven to 300 F.

2 In a large bowl, combine oats, nuts, cinnamon and salt. In a small bowl, stir together honey, maple syrup and vanilla. Pour over the oats and toss well to coat.

3 Spread mixture on a rimmed baking sheet and bake for about half an hour, stirring once or twice, until golden. Remove from oven and stir in the dried fruit. Let the granola cool completely on the baking sheet before transferring to an airtight container or individual zip-lock bags.

Makes about 8 cups.

Granola to Go

Remove granola from the oven and transfer to a large bowl to cool slightly. Reduce oven temperature to 225 F. Add 1/4 cup maple syrup and 2 egg whites to the granola and stir until well blended. Press about 1/2 cup of the mixture into each of 12 muffin tins (or divide among muffin tins) that have been sprayed with non-stick spray. Use the back of a spoon so it doesn't stick to your fingers. Bake for 20 minutes, until set.

Trail Mix

I know, trail mix is so obvious, who needs a recipe? But people rarely actually make it. My parents used to keep a glass jar of it on the countertop – a trend I think needs to make a comeback. Pretty much anything goes – trail mix keeps well and doesn't need to be refrigerated, so, like granola, you can keep zip-lock bags of it anywhere (I always have some in my gym bag, car and desk drawer.) Check out the bulk section of the grocery store for more ingredient ideas.

In a bowl combine any quantity of at least 4 of the following items. It's nice to have a combination of dried fruit, nuts and starch:

roasted peanuts
toasted almonds
pecan or walnut halves or pieces
toasted hazelnuts
soy nuts
pine nuts
cashews
toasted sunflower seeds
corn nuts
dried wasabi peas
raisins
dried cranberries
dried cherries
sliced dried apricots
sliced dried pears
dried apple slices
banana chips
chocolate chips
M&Ms minis
chocolate covered peanuts or raisins
mini marshmallows
pretzel sticks
sesame sticks
dry cereal - Multigrain Cheerios,
    Mini wheats, Shreddies, Chex, Sugar
    Crisp and Corn Bran all work well
granola (see page 18)

popcorn (plain, white cheese
    or light microwave)
caramel corn (see page 17)
crumbled graham crackers
Teddy Grahams
pretzel nuggets
bagel chips
mini goldfish crackers

Store in an airtight container or divide into individual zip-lock bags to keep on hand to grab and go! The nutritional value depends on what you use. If you're counting calories, go easy on the nut and chocolate ingredients.

Salted Edamame

Edamame is the Japanese name for soybeans which have been harvested early and left in the pod – they are easy to find fresh and frozen in Asian markets. Not only do soybeans contain a complete protein, they are a great source of all nine essential amino acids and are rich in calcium, iron, zinc and many of the B vitamins. Their antioxidant content protects against many forms of cancer, heart disease and osteoporosis and even lessens the unpleasant side effects of menopause. See? Snacking can be beneficial!

1 - 16 oz bag fresh or frozen edamame

1 Tbsp coarse sea salt

Contents per serving

Calories	196
Total fat	9.4 g
saturated fat	1.5 g
monounsaturated fat	2.2 g
polyunsaturated fat	5.7 g
Protein	18.9 g
Carbohydrates	11.2 g
Cholesterol	0.0 mg
Fiber	7.1 g
Calories from fat	43%

1 Bring a medium pot of salted water to a boil. Add the edamame and cook just until tender, which should take 3 - 4 minutes. Drain well and sprinkle generously with salt (leave them in their pods).

2 Serve in a bowl with a small empty bowl alongside for the pods.

Serves 4.

Because the flavor of the salt will predominate, use coarse sea salt or kosher salt, which has none of the additives (anti clumping agents, whiteners and iodine) of table salt. Sea salt is made by evaporating sea water, and much of its flavor comes from trace minerals – mostly calcium, magnesium and potassium. Kosher salt contains half the sodium of regular table salt.

Roasted Spiced Pumpkin Seeds

When it isn't pumpkin season you can often find the seeds in the bulk section at the grocery store. Pumpkin seeds are lower in fat than most other nuts and seeds, and a quarter of their weight is protein. They are also an excellent source of zinc, phosphorus, iron, fiber, potassium and magnesium.

2 cups fresh pumpkin seeds

1 Tbsp olive oil

1 tsp salt

1/2 tsp cayenne, curry powder, garam masala or chili powder

1/2 tsp cumin (optional)

1 Preheat oven to 350 F.

2 Wash the pumpkin seeds well and dry with paper towels. Toss in a small bowl with the oil and seasonings, and spread in a single layer on a cookie sheet.

3 Roast for 45 minutes, stirring occasionally, until crisp and golden.

Serves 6.

Contents per serving

Calories	115
Total fat	6.1 g
saturated fat	1.1 g
monounsaturated fat	2.9 g
polyunsaturated fat	2.1 g
Protein	4.0 g
Carbohydrates	11.5 g
Cholesterol	6.9 mg
Fiber	0.7 g
Calories from fat	48%

Spiced Maple Pecans

These keep well, so making a large batch will guarantee a good stash. They also make an excellent gift, bundled in cellophane or in an inexpensive glass jar tied with ribbon.

4 cups pecan halves (about a pound)

1/2 cup maple syrup

1 Tbsp sugar

1 tsp cumin

1 tsp chili powder

1 tsp paprika

1/2 tsp salt

pinch cayenne pepper (optional)

Contents per serving

Calories	268
Total fat	23.2 g
saturated fat	2.0 g
monounsaturated fat	15.2 g
polyunsaturated fat	6.0 g
Protein	2.9 g
Carbohydrates	13.6 g
Cholesterol	0.0 mg
Fiber	2.4 g
Calories from fat	77%

1 Preheat oven to 350 F.

2 Spread pecans in a single layer on a baking sheet and toast for 7 - 8 minutes, until fragrant. Drizzle with maple syrup and toss to coat; continue baking for another 10 minutes, stirring once or twice, until the nuts absorb most of the syrup.

3 In a small bowl, stir together the sugar, cumin, chili powder, paprika, salt and cayenne pepper. Sprinkle over the nuts and toss to coat. Spread on a cookie sheet to cool completely. Store in a tightly sealed container.

Serves 12.

Maple Cinnamon Pecans
Substitute the spice mix for a blend made with 1 Tbsp sugar, 1 tsp cinnamon, 1/2 tsp ginger and 1/2 tsp salt.

Garlic Pepper Pecans
Substitute the spice mix for a blend of 1 tsp garlic salt, 1/2 tsp paprika, 1/4 tsp freshly ground black pepper and a pinch of cayenne pepper.

Sue's Spiced Nuts

Even though they are high in calories, nuts are also high in protein, fiber, vitamins and minerals, so they make an excellent snack. Portion control is key. My friend Sue makes these addictive nuts all the time. They smell great while they're baking – even better than potpourri.

1 Tbsp olive oil or butter

1/2 tsp ground cumin

1/2 tsp chili powder

1/2 tsp garlic salt

1/4 tsp ground ginger

1/4 tsp cinnamon

1/4 tsp cayenne pepper

1/2 Tbsp coarse sea salt

2 cups unsalted mixed nuts

1 Preheat oven to 325 F.

2 Set a large saucepan over low heat and add oil and all the spices except the salt. Cook for a couple minutes, until the spices begin to toast. Add the nuts and cook, stirring, until well coated.

3 Transfer nuts to a baking sheet and bake for 15 minutes, shaking the pan occasionally so that they toast evenly. Toss with coarse salt and cool.

Makes 2 cups.

Contents per 1/3 cup

Calories	275
Total fat	25.4 g
saturated fat	2.3 g
monounsaturated fat	14.7 g
polyunsaturated fat	8.4 g
Protein	6.5 g
Carbohydrates	7.0 g
Cholesterol	0.0 mg
Fiber	3.1 g
Calories from fat	82%

Meringue Nuts

These nuts are lightly coated with a layer of meringue, which can be flavored any way you like. Use white sugar instead of brown, or try maple sugar if you can get your hands on some. Try adding 1 tsp Worcestershire sauce and 1 Tbsp sweet Hungarian paprika in place of the cinnamon.

2 cups mixed nuts, such as pecans, walnuts, cashews, almonds and hazelnuts

1 egg white

1/4 cup packed brown sugar

1 tsp cinnamon

few drops Tabasco sauce

1/2-1 tsp salt

Contents per 1/3 cup

Calories	285
Total fat	22.7 g
saturated fat	1.7 g
monounsaturated fat	10.2 g
polyunsaturated fat	10.8 g
Protein	7.1 g
Carbohydrates	15.1 g
Cholesterol	0.0 mg
Fiber	2.3 g
Calories from fat	71%

1. Preheat oven to 300 F.

2. In a medium bowl, beat egg white until foamy. Stir in nuts, sugar, cinnamon, Tabasco and salt.

3. Spread the mixture onto a baking sheet that has been sprayed with non-stick spray. Bake for 30 minutes, stirring occasionally, until golden. Cool on the pan.

Makes 2 cups.

Spiced Meringue Nuts

Add 2 tsp oregano and 1/2 tsp each chili powder, ground cumin and coriander in place of the cinnamon.

Sweet Spiced Pecans

These make an insanely decadent snack, and they are unbelievable sprinkled onto a salad! Nuts are an excellent source of healthy mono and polyunsaturated fats – the kind that lower your risk of heart disease – which make these an excellent alternative to chips. Just remember that the same healthy fats are also high in calories, so keep portions moderate. Because they are substantial, a small amount is satisfying.

2 cups pecan halves

2 Tbsp butter, melted

1 Tbsp packed brown sugar

1 tsp balsamic vinegar

2 drops hot sauce

1 Tbsp chopped fresh rosemary

1/2 tsp cumin (optional)

1/4 tsp cayenne pepper

1/2 tsp salt

a good grind of black pepper

1 Preheat the oven to 300 F.

2 Combine everything but the pecans in a medium bowl and stir well. Add the pecans and toss until well coated. Spread on a baking sheet.

3 Bake for 10 - 15 minutes, until golden.

Makes 2 cups.

Contents per 1/3 cup

Calories	285
Total fat	26.8 g
saturated fat	4.3 g
monounsaturated fat	16.3 g
polyunsaturated fat	6.2 g
Protein	2.9 g
Carbohydrates	9.2 g
Cholesterol	10.4 mg
Fiber	2.4 g
Calories from fat	84%

Honey Roasted Almonds

Nuts are nutritionally outstanding – they are a great source of protein, vitamins, minerals and monounsaturated fats, the kind that lowers cholesterol levels. People who eat nuts of all kinds regularly have a much lower risk of developing heart disease. Of all nuts, almonds contain the most calcium, and are 20% protein. Weight for weight, they contain 1/3 more protein than eggs!

3 cups whole almonds

1/2 cup honey

coarse salt to taste (optional)

Contents per 1/3 cup

Calories	351
Total fat	24.2 g
saturated fat	2.4 g
monounsaturated fat	16.5 g
polyunsaturated fat	5.3 g
Protein	9.9 g
Carbohydrates	27.2 g
Cholesterol	0.0 mg
Fiber	5.4 g
Calories from fat	61%

1 Preheat oven to 300 F. Line a rimmed cookie sheet with aluminum foil and spray the foil with non-stick spray.

2 In a medium saucepan, heat the honey until it is runny and easy to pour. Stir in the almonds along with any spices you like. Try adding 1 tsp Chinese five-spice powder or 1/2 tsp cayenne pepper to the honey to make Five Spice Almonds or Chili Honey Roasted Almonds.

3 Spread the honeyed almonds on the cookie sheet. Bake, stirring a couple of times, for about 40 minutes or until golden. Sprinkle with salt and set aside to cool.

Makes about 3 cups.

Honey Roasted Peppered Almonds & Pecans
Use half almonds, half pecans, and add 1 tsp coarse salt and freshly ground black pepper to the honey mixture.

Honey Roasted Nut & Seed Clusters

I used to bring granola bars and nuts along with me everywhere I went to fend off the temptation of fast food. Now I bring these clusters, which are sweet and salty, chewy and crunchy all at once. They are also an excellent source of protein, fiber, vitamins and minerals. Use any combination of nuts and seeds you like – I usually buy an assortment from the bulk section of the grocery store.

1¹/2 cups mixed nuts - sliced or slivered almonds, pine nuts, chopped pecans, hazelnuts, sunflower seeds, brazil nuts and walnuts all work well

¹/2 cup sesame seeds

2 Tbsp ground flaxseed (optional)

¹/4 cup honey

2 Tbsp water

¹/2 tsp canola oil

2 Tbsp sugar

1 tsp salt

1 Preheat oven to 350 F. Spread nuts and seeds on a baking sheet and toast for 8 - 10 minutes, shaking often, until pale golden and fragrant. Set aside.

2 In a medium saucepan, combine honey, water and oil. Bring to a boil over medium heat. Stir in nut mixture. Reduce heat to medium-low and cook, stirring, for another 2 minutes. Stir in sugar and salt and cook for another minute.

3 Spread the mixture in a thick layer on a cookie sheet and allow to cool. Once cooled, break it into clusters or as it cools squeeze it into balls while the mixture is still warm and pliable but cool enough to handle. Store in a tightly sealed container.

Serves 8.

Contents per serving

Calories	262
Total fat	17.6 g
saturated fat	1.7 g
monounsaturated fat	8.8 g
polyunsaturated fat	7.1 g
Protein	5.9 g
Carbohydrates	22.5 g
Cholesterol	0.0 mg
Fiber	2.8 g
Calories from fat	59%

Hot Soft Pretzels

This recipe may seem daunting but these are actually very simple to make, and a fun way to spend a Saturday morning if you have kids around. There is little actual work involved – most of the time is spent waiting for the dough to rise. And it's well worth the wait! Like bagels, pretzels are boiled first and then baked to produce a chewy texture inside and a crispy crust.

**1 package active dry yeast
(or 2^1/2 tsp if you buy it in bulk)**

1 Tbsp packed brown sugar

1 ^{1}/2 cups warm water (105 - 110 F)

1 tsp salt

**4 cups all-purpose flour, or 2 cups
all-purpose and 2 cups whole wheat**

extra flour for dusting work surface

coarse sea or kosher salt for sprinkling

Contents per pretzel

Calories	158
Total fat	0.4 g
saturated fat	0.1 g
monounsaturated fat	0.1 g
polyunsaturated fat	0.2 g
Protein	4.6 g
Carbohydrates	33.2 g
Cholesterol	0.0 mg
Fiber	1.5 g
Calories from fat	2%

1 In a large bowl combine yeast, half the brown sugar, and ^{1}/2 cup water and let stand 5 minutes until foamy. Add remaining sugar and water and stir well.

2 Add salt and 1 cup of the flour and stir until well blended. Add the remaining flour 1 cup at a time, mixing by hand until incorporated.

3 On a lightly floured surface, knead the dough for 5 - 7 minutes, until smooth and elastic. Transfer to a bowl, cover with a tea towel and let stand for 40 minutes in a warm place.

4 Dust your work surface with flour or cornmeal. Divide dough into 12 pieces and roll into long, ^{1}/2" thick ropes. Shape into pretzels, pressing ends to secure the dough.

5 Cover with a tea towel and let rise on the countertop or on a baking sheet for 20 - 30 minutes.

6 Preheat oven to 450 F.

7 Bring a large pot of water to a boil, and stir in ^{1}/2 tsp baking soda. Drop pretzels into the boiling water a couple at a time and cook for 1 minute, then flip and cook on the other side for a minute.

Garlic Peanuts

If you're a garlic fan, these may become a new addiction. You can buy raw peanuts in the bulk section of many grocery stores or in health food stores.

8 Using a slotted spoon, transfer pretzels to a baking sheet and sprinkle with coarse salt. Bake for 10 - 12 minutes, until golden.

Serve warm, on their own or drizzled with mustard. Makes 1 dozen pretzels.

Olive & Garlic Pretzels

Pulse 1/2 cup Kalamata olives, 2 cloves of garlic and, if you like, 1 anchovy fillet, in a food processor until finely chopped. Add to the yeast mixture along with the flour and proceed as directed.

Pizza Pretzels

Instead of sprinkling with salt, brush unbaked pretzels with tomato sauce and sprinkle with grated parmesan cheese. Bake as directed.

Pretzel Nuggets

Instead of shaping into pretzels, snip ropes of dough into 1" pieces and place on the baking sheet. Sprinkle with salt or dry ranch dip mix and bake as directed.

1 head garlic, peeled and crushed

1-2 Tbsp canola oil

2 cups raw peanuts

1 tsp salt

1 Combine garlic and canola oil in a large non-stick skillet and cook over medium heat, stirring constantly, until the garlic turns golden. Watch it carefully as it tends to burn quickly. Once it has turned golden, remove it from the oil with a fork and set aside in a small bowl.

2 Add the peanuts to the oil and cook over medium-low heat, stirring constantly, for 3 - 4 minutes or until golden.

3 Transfer to a bowl and toss with salt and the reserved garlic. Discard any remaining oil.

Makes 2 cups.

Contents per 1/4 cup

Calories	232
Total fat	18.8 g
saturated fat	2.6 g
monounsaturated fat	10.0 g
polyunsaturated fat	6.2 g
Protein	8.8 g
Carbohydrates	8.6 g
Cholesterol	0.0 mg
Fiber	3.3 g
Calories from fat	72%

Chewy Honey Energy Bars

In the same way homemade cookies taste far better than the packaged kind, homemade energy bars are better than any granola bar you can buy at the store. And cheaper! These are replicated from a minuscule bar on the market that retails for $1 each. Sunflower seeds are extremely nutritious, providing large quantities of protein, B vitamins, potassium, iron and zinc. Both sunflower and sesame seeds are among the best food sources of vitamin E. Sesame seeds are also an exceptional source of calcium, iron, niacin and folate. Truly virtuous grazing!

1 cup crushed Corn Flakes, Bran Flakes, Rice Krispies or Special K

1/2 cup raw or toasted hulled sunflower seeds

1/2 cup sesame seeds, toasted

1/4 cup sliced or slivered almonds, toasted

2 Tbsp flax seeds, ground (optional)

1/2 cup honey or Roger's Golden syrup

Contents per bar

Calories	164
Total fat	6.9 g
saturated fat	0.8 g
monounsaturated fat	2.7 g
polyunsaturated fat	3.4 g
Protein	3.3 g
Carbohydrates	23.7 g
Cholesterol	0.0 mg
Fiber	1.7 g
Calories from fat	37%

1. Combine all the ingredients except the honey in a medium bowl that has been sprayed with non-stick spray.

2. Bring honey to a boil in a small saucepan. Reduce heat to low and simmer for about 8 minutes, until the honey reaches 275 F (soft crack stage) on a candy thermometer. If you don't have a candy thermometer, pour a little of the hot syrup into ice water – it should separate into hard but pliable threads that bend slightly before breaking.

3. Pour over the cereal mixture and quickly stir to coat evenly.

4. Press the mixture into an 8" x 8" pan that has been sprayed with non-stick spray. Cool completely and cut into bars.

Makes 12 bars.

Peanut Butter & Honey Gorp

This peanut-buttery snack mix is a hit with kids; divide it among small zip-lock bags and keep a stash in the cupboard to throw in their lunches. Of course there's nothing keeping adults from scarfing it down as well.

¼ cup light or natural peanut butter

¼ cup honey or maple syrup

1 cup low fat granola
or any dry cereal you like

1 cup cinnamon Teddy Grahams
or crumbled graham crackers

1 cup stick pretzels

1 cup dried fruit, such as raisins,
cranberries and slivered apricots

Contents per serving

Calories	192
Total fat	3.9 g
saturated fat	0.9 g
monounsaturated fat	1.9 g
polyunsaturated fat	1.1 g
Protein	3.5 g
Carbohydrates	37.0 g
Cholesterol	0.0 mg
Fiber	2.5 g
Calories from fat	19%

1. Preheat oven to 300 F.

2. Combine the peanut butter and honey in a small microwave-safe bowl. Microwave at high for 30 seconds or until melted; stir until smooth. Place granola, Teddy Grahams and pretzels in a large bowl; pour peanut butter mixture over granola mixture and toss to coat.

3. Spread the mixture on a cookie sheet and bake for 20 minutes, stirring once or twice. Remove from the oven and stir in raisins and cranberries. Cool completely on the pan. Store in a tightly sealed container.

Makes 4 cups; serves about 8.

Caramel Crunch

OK, it may be obvious by now that I am a big fan of crunchy caramel things. This is what you'd end up with if party mix got together with caramel corn.

3/4 cup packed brown sugar

1/4 cup corn syrup

1 Tbsp butter or margarine

pinch salt

1 bag popped low fat buttery microwave popcorn

2 cups Cheerios, Chex, Shreddies, puffed wheat or any dry cereal you like

2 cups stick pretzels

2 cups animal crackers, Teddy Grahams or crumbled graham crackers

Contents per serving

Calories	219
Total fat	3.5 g
saturated fat	1.0 g
monounsaturated fat	0.7 g
polyunsaturated fat	0.3 g
Protein	2.5 g
Carbohydrates	45.8 g
Cholesterol	3.9 mg
Fiber	0.6 g
Calories from fat	14%

1. Preheat oven to 350 F.

2. Combine popcorn, cereals, pretzels and crackers in a large bowl that has been sprayed with non-stick spray.

3. Combine brown sugar, corn syrup, butter and salt in a small saucepan over medium heat and cook, stirring constantly, until melted and smooth. Pour over the popcorn mixture and quickly toss to coat.

4. Spread the mixture onto a rimmed baking sheet or into a 9" x 13" pan and bake for 20 - 30 minutes, until golden. Cool in the pan before serving.

Serves 8.

Maple Crunch

Substitute maple syrup for the corn syrup, and add 1 tsp maple extract if you have it.

Peanut Butter & Honey Crunch

Instead of the caramel, melt 1/2 cup each light peanut butter and honey together on the stovetop or in the microwave. Pour over popcorn mixture and stir to coat. Bake and cool as directed. If you like, add a handful of raisins or dried fruit after baking. For PB & J Crunch substitute raspberry jam for the honey. You don't need to bake this kind, but let it cool down before serving.

Sesame Snaps

When I was little, sesame snaps and sponge toffee were my favorite treats to get when we went to the grocery store. You can still buy the same little blue and white packages of it by the checkout, but homemade is easy and much tastier. This recipe can easily be halved or doubled.

1/2 cup sesame seeds

1/2 cup sugar

1/2 cup honey or Roger's Golden Syrup

Contents per piece

Calories	50
Total fat	2.8 g
saturated fat	0.4 g
monounsaturated fat	1.1 g
polyunsaturated fat	1.3 g
Protein	1.1 g
Carbohydrates	8.3 g
Cholesterol	0.0 mg
Fiber	0.6 g
Calories from fat	42%

1 Combine sugar and honey in a medium-large heavy saucepan. Stir over medium heat until the sugar dissolves. Continue to cook without stirring until the caramel turns light golden, swirling the pan occasionally. Add the sesame seeds and continue to cook in the same manner until the mixture turns deep golden. Watch it carefully – sugar burns fast!

2 Pour the mixture onto a cookie sheet that has been sprayed with non-stick spray or lined with a silpat mat. Immediately tilt the pan to make it spread as thin as possible – do it quickly because the edges begin to cool first. If you need help, use the back of a spoon that has been rubbed with a little oil.

3 Set it aside to cool. Once it has cooled, break into chunks. Store in a tightly sealed container, especially if you live somewhere humid!

Makes about 24 - 2" pieces.

Crackers & Crisps

Practically everyone bakes cookies, so why not crackers? Like cookies, they are far better homemade than store-bought. They are inexpensive, easy to make and you can flavor them any way you like. Crackers are more than just vehicles for cheeses and dips – they make great snacks on their own. Try giving crackers to young kids instead of cookies to keep them happy. You'll feel better knowing they have no additives or preservatives.

Basic Crackers

Everyone makes cookies at home, so why not crackers? This is a great basic cracker recipe to use as a blank canvas - experiment with different kinds of flours and flavorings such as herbs, spices, citrus zest, seeds, nuts and grated sharp cheeses. To make tart shells, press cut out cracker dough into mini muffin cups and bake until golden, then cool and fill with whatever you like.

2 cups flour, or 1 cup all purpose flour and 1 cup whole wheat, rye or spelt flour

1 tsp sugar

1/2 tsp salt

2 Tbsp butter or stick margarine, chilled

3/4 cup water, milk or buttermilk

Any additions you like, such as coarse salt, sesame, poppy, fennel or caraway seed, dehydrated garlic, freshly ground pepper, Parmesan cheese or chopped fresh rosemary

Contents per cracker

Calories	23
Total fat	0.4 g
saturated fat	0.3 g
monounsaturated fat	0.1 g
polyunsaturated fat	0.0 g
Protein	0.5 g
Carbohydrates	4.1 g
Cholesterol	1.3 mg
Fiber	0.2 g
Calories from fat	20%

1. Preheat oven to 350 F.

2. Combine the flour, sugar, salt and butter in the bowl of a food processor and pulse until well blended. Add the water or milk and pulse until you have a soft dough.

3. On a lightly floured surface, roll the dough out about 1/8" thick. Sprinkle with any flavorings you like and roll gently with the rolling pin to help the toppings adhere.

4. Cut into squares, rectangles, or rounds with a pizza wheel, pastry cutter, cookie cutter or knife and transfer to an ungreased cookie sheet. Reroll the scraps only once to get as many crackers as you can.

5. Bake for 15 - 20 minutes, until golden. Transfer to a wire rack to cool and store in a tightly sealed container.

Makes about 4 dozen crackers.

Buttermilk Cumin Crackers
Use half all purpose and half whole wheat flour, add 1 tsp ground cumin to the mixture and use buttermilk instead of water.

Lemon Poppyseed Crackers
Add the grated zest of one lemon, 2 Tbsp poppyseed and a generous pinch of pepper to the flour mixture.

Flaxseed Wafers

These are my favorite crackers. Flaxseed is the richest known source of plant lignans (phytoestrogens), containing about 500 times more than soybeans! They are also a great source of soluble and insoluble fiber, and have a deliciously nutty taste. What better food to snack on? It's important to mention, however, that because they are so teeny and hard they cannot be digested unless they are well-chewed or ground, so it's a good idea to give them a turn in a coffee mill or spice grinder or they'll just pass right on through...

1 large egg

1 Tbsp olive or canola oil

2 Tbsp water

1 cup flour (all purpose or whole wheat)

1/4 tsp salt

1/2 cup flaxseed or sesame seeds

coarse salt, for sprinkling (optional)

Contents per cracker

Calories	59
Total fat	2.5 g
saturated fat	0.3 g
monounsaturated fat	1.0 g
polyunsaturated fat	1.2 g
Protein	1.9 g
Carbohydrates	7.1 g
Cholesterol	12.0 mg
Fiber	1.0 g
Calories from fat	40%

1. Preheat oven to 350 F.

2. Pulse the flaxseed in a coffee or spice grinder until coarsely chopped – its necessary if you want to reap their nutritional benefits! In a medium bowl, stir together the egg, oil and water. Add the flour, salt and flaxseed and stir until you have a stiff dough.

3. Pinch off 1" balls of dough and roll them out on the countertop back and forth in one direction as thin as you can. Don't flour the countertop – this works much better when they can cling to the surface and end up a nice, even, rustic-looking smear. You can get them really thin that way. If you want them salty, sprinkle with coarse salt and roll to help it adhere. Peel them off the counter and place on an ungreased cookie sheet.

4. Bake for 12 - 15 minutes, until golden and crisp.

Makes about 18 large crackers.

Sesame Parmesan Crackers
Add 2 Tbsp grated Parmesan cheese along with the flour, and use sesame seeds instead of flaxseed.

Cheddar Sesame Crackers

Whole wheat flour gives these a nutty flavor and adds fiber, but use all purpose if you like. Old cheddar has a much more intense flavor than the medium or mild varieties, so you don't need as much of it.

1 cup whole wheat flour

1/2 cup grated old cheddar cheese

pinch salt

2 Tbsp canola oil

1/2 cup water

sesame seeds for sprinkling

Contents per cracker

Calories	14
Total fat	0.8 g
saturated fat	0.2 g
monounsaturated fat	0.4 g
polyunsaturated fat	0.2 g
Protein	0.5 g
Carbohydrates	1.5 g
Cholesterol	0.5 mg
Fiber	0.3 g
Calories from fat	47%

1 Preheat oven to 375 F.

2 Combine the flour, cheese and salt in the bowl of a food processor and pulse until well blended. Add the oil and pulse again. (Alternately, use a fork or whisk in a regular bowl). Add the water and pulse until it looks well blended and crumbly.

3 Turn the mixture out onto a lightly floured surface and gather it into a ball. Roll the dough out about 1/8" thick; sprinkle with sesame seeds and roll again to help them adhere.

4 Cut into 1" squares with a pizza cutter or knife. Place on an ungreased cookie sheet and prick each cracker with a fork. Bake for about 20 minutes, until golden.

Makes about 5 dozen 1" crackers.

Rosemary Raisin Pecan Crisps

I, like so many other Canadians, have recently become hooked on Lesley Stowe's rosemary pecan Raincoast Crisps, which quickly turned into an expensive addiction! After devouring the last box (with really good aged Gouda, and without sharing) I became determined to develop a recipe so I could make them on my own. I looked at the ingredients on the box and altered a basic recipe for Boston brown bread. Voila!

2 cups flour

2 tsp baking soda

1 tsp salt

2 cups buttermilk

1/4 cup brown sugar

1/4 cup honey

1 cup raisins

1/2 cup chopped pecans

1/2 cup roasted pumpkin seeds (optional)

1/4 cup sesame seeds

1/4 cup flaxseed, ground

1 Tbsp chopped fresh rosemary

Contents per crisp

Calories	30
Total fat	0.8 g
saturated fat	0.1 g
monounsaturated fat	0.4 g
polyunsaturated fat	0.3 g
Protein	0.7 g
Carbohydrates	5.3 g
Cholesterol	0.2 mg
Fiber	0.3 g
Calories from fat	23%

1. Preheat oven to 350 F.

2. In a large bowl, stir together the flour, baking soda and salt. Add the buttermilk, brown sugar and honey and stir a few strokes. Add the raisins, pecans, pumpkin seeds, sesame seeds, flaxseed and rosemary and stir just until blended.

3. Pour the batter into two 4" x 8" loaf pans that have been sprayed with non-stick spray. Bake for about 45 minutes, until golden and springy to the touch. Remove from the pans and cool on a wire rack.

4. The cooler the bread, the easier it is to slice really thin. You can leave it until the next day or pop it in the freezer. Slice the loaves as thin as you can and place the slices in a single layer on an ungreased cookie sheet. I like to slice and bake one loaf and pop the other in the freezer for later. Reduce the oven heat to 300 F and bake them for about 15 minutes, then flip them over and bake for another 10 minutes, until crisp and deep golden. Try not to eat them all at once.

Makes about 8 dozen crackers.

Wheat Thins

These are really simple, plain crackers to make and to eat. Canola oil has the lowest concentration of saturated fat of all cooking oils, which makes these much healthier than the store-bought kind. Canola oil has a neutral flavor – try substituting walnut or hazelnut oil for a different taste.

1^1/2 cups flour

1^1/2 cups whole wheat flour

^{1}/2 tsp salt

^{1}/4 cup canola oil

1 cup water

Coarse salt, for sprinkling (optional)

Contents per cracker

Calories	18
Total fat	0.5 g
saturated fat	0.0 g
monounsaturated fat	0.3 g
polyunsaturated fat	0.2 g
Protein	0.5 g
Carbohydrates	2.9 g
Cholesterol	0.0 mg
Fiber	0.3 g
Calories from fat	28%

1. In a medium bowl, stir together the flours and salt. Add the canola oil and water and mix until you have a soft dough. Divide the dough in half and let it rest for about 15 minutes.

2. Preheat oven to 350 F.

3. On a lightly floured surface, roll the dough into a rectangle as thin as possible - no thicker than ^{1}/8". Sprinkle with salt and roll to help it adhere.

4. Place the whole thing on an ungreased baking sheet and cut into squares with a pizza wheel or knife; don't bother to separate them. Prick each cracker a few times with a fork.

5. Bake for 15 - 20 minutes, until golden and crisp. Cool and break into squares.

Makes about 8 dozen 1^1/2" crackers.

Flax Wheat Thins
Add 2 Tbsp ground flaxseed to the flour mixture, or sprinkle on top along with the salt.

Tomato Basil Wheat Thins
Use tomato or V-8 juice in place of the water, and add 1 tsp dried basil to the flour.

Garlic Roasted Potato Skins

I realize these don't exactly fit into the 'cracker' category, but they make great, sturdy scoopers for any kind of dip, and have nutritional benefits from the potato skins. Potato chips make great dippers too, especially when you slice the potatoes lengthwise and leave the skins on. The recipe is on page 12.

4 medium russet (baking) potatoes

1 head garlic

1 - 2 Tbsp olive or canola oil

salt and pepper to taste

Contents per potato skin

Calories	38
Total fat	0.8 g
saturated fat	0.1 g
monounsaturated fat	0.6 g
polyunsaturated fat	0.1 g
Protein	1.0 g
Carbohydrates	6.9 g
Cholesterol	0.0 mg
Fiber	0.6 g
Calories from fat	20%

1. Preheat oven to 350 F.

2. Prick each potato once or twice with a fork. Cut a thin slice off the top of the head of garlic and wrap the head in tin foil. Bake the garlic and potatoes for about an hour, until the potatoes are tender. Remove from oven and set the potatoes on a rack until they are cool enough to handle. Open the foil and let the garlic cool. Turn the oven up to 450 F. (Everything can be prepared up to this point and refrigerated for 24 hours, until you're ready to bake them.)

3. Quarter the potatoes lengthwise and scoop out the flesh (keep it for another use – it makes great home fries the next day!), leaving 1/4" thick skins.

4. Squeeze the roasted garlic into a small bowl and mash it with a fork, adding the oil, salt and pepper. Mash until you have a paste. Spread the paste generously onto the potato skins and transfer to a baking sheet.

5. Bake for 20 - 25 minutes, until golden.

   Makes 16 potato skins.

Pita Chips

If you want to cut back the fat even further, omit the oil and spray the pitas lightly with non-stick spray to help the seasonings adhere. Or bake them absolutely plain. If you're cooking outside, grill whole split, seasoned pitas until grill-marked and crisp, then break into wedges.

3 pita bread rounds, white or whole wheat

1 Tbsp olive or canola oil (optional)

1 clove garlic, crushed (optional)

Onion or garlic powder, freshly ground black pepper, lemon pepper, basil, dried Italian seasoning, grated Parmesan cheese, 5 spice powder or any other herb or spice you like

Contents per chip

Calories	13
Total fat	0.2 g
saturated fat	0.0 g
monounsaturated fat	0.2 g
polyunsaturated fat	0.0 g
Protein	0.3 g
Carbohydrates	2.1 g
Cholesterol	0.0 mg
Fiber	0.1 g
Calories from fat	22%

1. Preheat oven to 400 F.

2. Split pitas in half around the edge so that you have two circles. Stir the garlic into the oil and brush the rough side of the pitas lightly with it. Stack them and cut into 8 wedges with a knife or pizza wheel.

3. Place pita wedges on a cookie sheet and sprinkle with your choice of flavorings. They are just as good left plain.

4. Bake for 5 - 7 minutes, until golden and crisp. Store extras in a tightly sealed container.

Makes 2 dozen chips.

Curried Pita Chips
Mix 1/2 tsp curry powder or paste, 1/4 tsp ground cumin and a pinch of cayenne pepper into 1 Tbsp canola oil and brush over the pita chips before baking.

Bagel Chips

This is a great way to resurrect stale bagels! Plain bagel chips make perfect scoops for thick dips and spreads, but if you want them to have flavor on their own, use onion or garlic bagels or toss them with a bit of oil and some flavorings before you bake them.

Bagels, any flavor

1 tsp canola or olive oil per bagel (optional)

Any seasonings you choose – coarse salt, sesame seed, Parmesan cheese, herbs or powdered ranch dressing mix

1 Preheat oven to 350 F.

2 Slice bagels vertically into thin round slices and place on a cookie sheet. Bake for 5 - 7 minutes, until golden.

Olive Oil & Garlic Bagel Chips

Stir a clove of crushed garlic into 1 Tbsp olive oil and toss the chips in it to coat well before baking. (This is enough for 2 bagels.)

Contents per slice

Calories	10
Total fat	0.0 g
Protein	0.4 g
Carbohydrates	2.1 g
Cholesterol	1.0 mg
Fiber	0.0 g
Calories from fat	6 %

Crostini

Cut the baguette on a slight diagonal so that they're easier to bite into.

1 baguette, sliced diagonally about 1/2" thick

1 Tbsp - 1/4 cup olive oil

1 large clove garlic, cut in half lengthwise

1 Preheat oven to 350 F.

2 Place the baguette slices on a cookie sheet and brush them lightly with olive oil. Toast for about 10 minutes, until pale golden around the edges. Rub the toasts with the cut side of the garlic clove while they're still warm.

Makes about 4 dozen crostini, depending on the size of your baguette.

Contents per slice

Calories	14
Total fat	0.2 g
saturated fat	0.0 g
monounsaturated fat	0.2 g
polyunsaturated fat	0.0 g
Protein	0.4 g
Carbohydrates	2.6 g
Cholesterol	0.0 mg
Fiber	0.2 g
Calories from fat	18%

Wonton Crisps

If you're looking for something to replace potato chips, this is it. Wontons make crispy, low fat snacks and are sturdy enough to scoop up loads of dip. They're cheap too – one package of wonton wrappers costs a little over a dollar and makes about 14 dozen crisps! All you need to do is cut the wontons in half into strips or triangles and bake them with your choice of seasoning. I love them with just salt and pepper.

Fresh wonton wrappers
(2 - 4 dozen or half a package)

Non-stick spray or canola oil

Sesame, Garlic & Parmesan

1 Tbsp sesame seeds (optional)

1 Tbsp grated Parmesan cheese

1 tsp salt

1/2 tsp garlic powder

Cinnamon Sugar

1 Tbsp sugar

1/4 tsp ground cinnamon

Spicy Curry

2 tsp curry powder

1/2 tsp salt

1/4 tsp each cumin, paprika and garlic powder

pinch freshly ground black pepper

Salt and Pepper

1/2 tsp each salt and freshly ground black pepper

1 Preheat oven to 350 F.

2 Combine seasoning ingredients in a small bowl.

3 Cut stack of wontons diagonally into triangles or across into strips, then separate them onto a cookie sheet. Lightly spray them with non-stick spray or brush them lightly with canola or olive oil. Sprinkle with your choice of seasoning mixture.

4 Bake for 5 minutes or until deep golden and crisp. Watch carefully – they darken fast!

Contents per chip

Calories	12
Total fat	0.0 g
Protein	0.4 g
Carbohydrates	2.3 g
Cholesterol	0.4 mg
Fiber	0.0 g
Calories from fat	8%

Flour Tortillas

Homemade tortillas are truly easy, cheap and far superior to the store bought kind. If you prefer whole wheat tortillas, use half whole wheat flour.

2 cups flour

1/2 tsp baking powder

1/4 tsp salt

2 Tbsp canola oil

2/3 - 3/4 cup warm water

Contents per tortilla

Calories	144
Total fat	3.4 g
saturated fat	0.3 g
monounsaturated fat	2.0 g
polyunsaturated fat	1.1 g
Protein	3.2 g
Carbohydrates	23.8 g
Cholesterol	0.0 mg
Fiber	1.0 g
Calories from fat	24%

1 In a large mixing bowl, combine the flour, baking powder, salt, oil and half the water. Stir and continue adding water until the dough comes together but is not too sticky. Knead on a lightly floured surface for about 5 minutes, until the dough is smooth and elastic.

2 If you have time at this point, cover the dough and let it sit at room temperature for half an hour (or up to several hours) to let it relax.

3 Divide the dough into 8 balls. On a lightly floured surface, press each ball into a disc and then roll it out as thin as possible – it should be about 7" - 8" in diameter.

4 Cook the tortillas one at a time in a dry skillet set over medium heat, until it blisters and brown spots begin to appear. It should take about a minute per side. Serve warm and store extras tightly wrapped.

Makes 8 tortillas.

Mini Flour Tortillas

Pinch off 3/4" balls of dough and press with the back of a spatula to flatten. Bake several at a time as directed. Makes about 50 tortillas with 23 calories and half a gram of fat each.

Cinnamon Sugar Tortilla Chips

Homemade baked tortilla chips are far yummier and crunchier than the packaged baked tortilla chips, which don't have much flavor.

2 - 8" flour tortillas,
store bought or home made (see page 45)

1 egg white

1 Tbsp sugar

1/4 tsp cinnamon

Contents per chip

Calories	14
Total fat	0.2 g
saturated fat	0.0 g
monounsaturated fat	0.1 g
polyunsaturated fat	0.1 g
Protein	0.4 g
Carbohydrates	2.4 g
Cholesterol	0.0 mg
Fiber	0.1 g
Calories from fat	19%

1. Preheat oven to 350 F.

2. Combine the sugar and cinnamon in a small bowl. Beat the egg white with about 1 Tbsp of water until foamy and lightly brush both sides of tortillas. Sprinkle each side with the sugar mixture.

3. Cut each tortilla into 8 wedges and bake on a cookie sheet for 8 - 10 minutes, until golden and crisp. If you like, serve with fruit salsa and sour cream sweetened with brown sugar.

Makes 16 chips.

Baked Tortilla Chips

To make plain tortilla chips, all you need to do is cut flour tortillas into wedges or strips; place them on a cookie sheet and bake at 350 F for 10 minutes or until crisp

Chili Lime Corn Chips

If you can find fresh corn tortillas, these make a delicious alternative to Doritos.

12 corn tortillas

2 Tbsp lime juice

1 tsp coarse sea salt

1/2 tsp chili powder

1/2 tsp cumin

1 Preheat oven to 350 F.

2 Combine the salt, chili powder and cumin in a small dish. Brush the tortillas with lime juice and sprinkle with the spice mixture. Stack a few at a time and cut into 6 wedges using a knife or pizza cutter.

3 Place the chips in a single layer on an ungreased baking sheet and bake for 10 minutes, or until crisp.

Makes about 72 chips.

Contents per chip

Calories	9
Total fat	0.0 g
Protein	0.2 g
Carbohydrates	2.0 g
Cholesterol	0.0 mg
Fiber	0.2 g
Calories from fat	9%

Parmesan Toasts

These make great vehicles for dips, or serve them alone with a dish of good olives to nibble before dinner.

12 baguette slices, cut on the diagonal

1/2 cup grated Parmesan cheese

2 Tbsp milk

2 Tbsp chopped fresh parsley

pinch cayenne pepper

1 Preheat oven to 450 F.

2 In a small bowl, stir together the Parmesan cheese, milk, parsley and cayenne pepper. Spread on the toasts and place on a baking sheet.

3 Bake for 5 - 10 minutes, until golden and the cheese has melted.

Makes 12 toasts.

Contents per toast

Calories	33
Total fat	1.2 g
saturated fat	0.8 g
monounsaturated fat	0.4 g
polyunsaturated fat	0.0 g
Protein	2.2 g
Carbohydrates	2.9 g
Cholesterol	3.4 mg
Fiber	0.1 g
Calories from fat	36%

Quick Breadsticks

When you need fresh breadsticks fast, this dough can be mixed up in a food processor in 2 minutes. Serve your breadsticks in a tall glass or small vase.

1 cup flour

1 cup whole wheat flour

2 tsp baking powder

1/2 tsp salt

3 Tbsp olive or canola oil

1/2 - 3/4 cup water or milk

Coarse salt (optional)

Contents per stick

Calories	51
Total fat	1.8 g
saturated fat	0.3 g
monounsaturated fat	1.3 g
polyunsaturated fat	0.2 g
Protein	1.2 g
Carbohydrates	7.7 g
Cholesterol	0.0 mg
Fiber	0.8 g
Calories from fat	31%

1. Preheat oven to 400 F.

2. Combine the flour, baking powder and salt in the bowl of a food processor and pulse to combine. Add the oil and pulse until the mixture resembles coarse meal.

3. With the machine running, pour 1/2 - 3/4 cup of cold water or milk through the feed tube and process until the dough comes together. I usually need 1/2 cup plus about 2 Tbsp of liquid.

4. On a lightly floured surface, roll the dough out about 1/8" thick. Sprinkle with salt if you like, and roll lightly to help it adhere. Cut into 1/2" - 3/4" wide strips as long or short as you like, then twist the strips into rustic looking sticks.

5. Place the sticks on an ungreased baking sheet and press the ends onto the sheet if they start to unravel. Bake for 12 - 15 minutes, or until golden.

Makes about 2 dozen breadsticks.

Pesto Breadsticks
Add a spoonful of pesto along with the oil.

Olive & Garlic Breadsticks
Whiz 1/4 cup Kalamata olives and a clove of garlic along with the flour mixture.

Rosemary Parmesan Twists

These crunchy twists are delicious on their own, and go really well with all kinds of dip. Try making elegant olive or sun dried tomato twists by replacing the rosemary with a few chopped black olives or sun dried tomatoes.

1 cup flour

3/4 cup whole wheat flour

1/4 cup fresh rosemary
(pull the leaves off the twigs)

1/4 cup grated Parmesan cheese

1/2 tsp salt

2 Tbsp canola or olive oil

1/2 cup water

coarse salt for sprinkling (optional)

Contents per stick

Calories	58
Total fat	1.8 g
saturated fat	0.4 g
monounsaturated fat	0.9 g
polyunsaturated fat	0.5 g
Protein	1.8 g
Carbohydrates	8.5 g
Cholesterol	1.0 mg
Fiber	0.8 g
Calories from fat	31%

1. Preheat oven to 400 F.

2. In the bowl of a food processor, combine the flours, rosemary, Parmesan cheese and salt until well blended and the rosemary is chopped. With the motor running, pour the oil and water through the feed tube and process until well blended. Gather the dough into a ball; cover with a tea towel and let it rest for 15 minutes.

3. On a lightly floured surface, roll the dough out into a rectangle about 1/8" thick – it should be about 10" x 16". If you like, sprinkle with salt and roll to help it adhere.

4. With a sharp knife or pizza wheel, cut the dough crosswise into 1/2" wide strips. Twist each strip a few times and place on an ungreased baking sheet. (Press the ends to the sheet if they begin to unravel.) Bake for 15 - 20 minutes, until golden.

Makes about 20 twists.

Dip, Spread, Dunk & Smear

There's something childlike and indulgent about dipping one food into another. I confess I am more a scooper than a dipper... the goal for me is to get as much dip onto my cracker or veg as it can structurally tolerate.

People think dips are just for parties, but Tupperware and zip-lock baggies make them just as portable as anything else. Hummus is one of my favorite lunches to eat at my desk or take on road trips with torn up pitas and fresh veggies. Mix up a dip instead of popcorn when you're watching a movie, or put some out on the table when the kids are doing their homework or everyone comes to play Scrabble. Dip makes a great motivational tool to get vegetable haters to eat their veggies, but try dunking fruit, flatbread, breadsticks, baked tortilla chips, potato skins and crackers too. Most dips keep very well in the fridge, so don't be afraid to make a big batch.

Spinach & Artichoke Dip

This is perfect for any gathering that requires food, but I've been known to make a batch even when I'm alone. It's worth making even for one – cold leftovers are delicious spread on a bagel and make an unbelievable omelette filling! If you're having a party, you can make this ahead and keep it in the fridge until you're ready to pop it in the oven.

1 small onion, finely chopped

2 cloves garlic, crushed

1 - 10 oz package frozen chopped spinach, thawed with excess moisture squeezed out

1 - 14 oz (398 mL) can artichoke hearts, drained and chopped, reserving the liquid

1 - 8 oz (250 g) package light cream cheese, cubed

1/2 cup milk

1 cup low fat sour cream

1/2 cup grated Parmesan cheese

salt and pepper to taste

1 cup shredded part skim mozzarella cheese (optional)

Contents per serving

Calories	169
Total fat	8.6 g
saturated fat	5.5 g
monounsaturated fat	2.7 g
polyunsaturated fat	0.4 g
Protein	10.1 g
Carbohydrates	12.8 g
Cholesterol	29 mg
Fiber	3.3 g
Calories from fat	48%

1. Preheat oven to 350 F.

2. Spray a medium non-stick skillet with non-stick spray. Add the onions, garlic and about 1 Tbsp of artichoke liquid; sauté until the onion is tender but not browned, adding more liquid if you need it. Add the spinach and sauté until all the liquid has evaporated.

3. Reduce heat to low and stir in the artichokes, cream cheese and milk. Cook, stirring constantly, until the cheese melts. Stir in the sour cream, Parmesan cheese, salt and pepper and cook until it's heated through.

4. If you want to serve the dip as is, transfer it to a bowl and serve it while it's warm. If you want to bake it, spoon the mixture into a shallow baking dish or pie plate. Sprinkle with remaining mozzarella cheese and bake for about 30 minutes, until golden and bubbly. Serve with tortilla chips and veggies.

Serves 8.

Crab, Spinach & Artichoke Dip
Stir a drained can of crabmeat into the spinach mixture.

Caesar or Salsa Spinach & Artichoke Dip
Stir 1/2 cup light creamy Caesar dressing or 1 cup chunky salsa into the spinach mixture.

Hot Crab & Artichoke Dip

There's no reason in the world that you should stop eating gooey crab dip packed with cheese – just make sure you don't polish off the whole thing yourself. Omit the artichokes if you want just a cheesy crab dip, or replace it with half a package of frozen spinach, thawed, with the extra moisture squeezed out. If it seems too thick for your taste, thin it with a little milk.

1 - 8oz (250 g) tub light cream cheese

1 cup low fat sour cream

2 Tbsp lemon juice

1 Tbsp grated onion (purple onion looks nice)

1 tsp Worcestershire sauce

1 clove garlic, crushed

2 - 3 dashes hot pepper sauce (optional)

1/2 tsp dry mustard

salt and pepper to taste

1/2 - 1 lb. lump crabmeat, cartilage removed (or 2 – 170g cans, drained)

1 - 14 oz (398 mL) can artichoke hearts, drained and chopped

1/2 cup grated old cheddar cheese

1. Preheat oven to 350 F.

2. In a large bowl, beat cream cheese until smooth. Stir in sour cream, lemon juice, onion, Worcestershire sauce, garlic, hot sauce, mustard, salt and pepper. Stir in the crabmeat, artichoke hearts and cheese.

3. Spoon into a shallow baking dish or pie plate and bake for 20 - 30 minutes, until heated through and bubbly around the edges. Serve warm with baked tortillas, crackers, pita or bagel chips or fresh veggies.

Serves 8.

Contents per serving

Calories	165
Total fat	7.8 g
saturated fat	4.8 g
monounsaturated fat	2.5 g
polyunsaturated fat	0.5 g
Protein	12.3 g
Carbohydrates	10.2 g
Cholesterol	41.4 mg
Fiber	2.3 g
Calories from fat	46%

Caramelized Onion Dip

Chips and dip is one of my Mom's few vices (which all involve food and a certain soft drink that will remain nameless). If you want to do it right (and you might as well if you're going to indulge), try homemade chips (see page 12) with this dip. Dips made with those packets of French onion soup mix are loaded with salt and additives – this recipe is much healthier... and tastier too! Sometimes I add a few tablespoons of beef stock to the onions while they are caramelizing to add flavor, and as an alternative to adding more oil. If you want your dip extra rich, stir a few spoonfuls of light cream cheese into the mixture along with the sour cream.

1 Tbsp canola or olive oil

3 large sweet onions (such as Vidalia or Walla Walla) or yellow onions, cut in half and thinly sliced

2 cloves garlic, crushed

1 Tbsp balsamic vinegar

1 cup low fat sour cream

salt and pepper to taste

Contents per 1/4 cup

Calories	81
Total fat	4.1 g
saturated fat	1.4 g
monounsaturated fat	1.9 g
polyunsaturated fat	0.8 g
Protein	2.6 g
Carbohydrates	8.0 g
Cholesterol	6.7 mg
Fiber	0.6 g
Calories from fat	47%

1. Heat oil in a large non-stick skillet over medium-low heat. Add the onions and cook, stirring often, for about 20 minutes, until they turn golden. Add the garlic and balsamic vinegar and cook for another 3 minutes, until deep golden and caramelized. Set aside to cool slightly.

2. Transfer to a medium bowl and stir in sour cream, salt and pepper. If you want, whiz it all in a food processor until smooth. Cover and chill for at least an hour before serving.

Makes about 1 1/2 cups.

Caramelized Onion & Spinach Dip
Add 1/2 lb baby spinach, coarsely chopped or 1/2 package frozen chopped spinach, thawed and squeezed dry, to the skillet along with the balsamic vinegar. Cook for a few extra minutes to wilt the spinach and cook off any excess moisture.

Warm Chevre Dip
Omit the sour cream. After adding the vinegar, add a few spoonfuls of light cream cheese to the pan along with 1/4 cup each soft goat cheese, chopped sun-dried tomatoes, Kalamata olives and artichoke hearts. Stir to heat through and serve warm.

Chili Con Queso Dip

I'm not a fan of low fat cheeses – they tend to have a rubbery texture and little flavor. I much prefer sharp cheeses such as old cheddar, which is intensely flavored so that a little goes a long way! Add a small can of chopped green chilies if you want to spice this up.

1 tsp canola or olive oil

1 small onion, chopped

2 cloves garlic, crushed

1 Tbsp flour

1 - 14 oz (398 mL) can diced tomatoes, undrained

1 cup salsa

1/2 - 1 tsp chili powder

salt and pepper to taste

1/2 - 8 oz (250 g) package light cream cheese, cubed

1 cup grated old cheddar cheese

1 Heat the oil in a large non-stick skillet and sauté the onions and garlic until soft. Add the flour and cook for another minute – the mixture will be dry. Add the diced tomatoes, salsa, chili powder, salt and pepper and bring to a simmer.

2 Reduce heat to low and add the cream cheese. Stir until it's almost melted, then add the grated cheddar and stir until all the cheese is melted and smooth.

3 Serve warm with baked tortilla chips.

Serves about 8.

Spinach Con Queso Dip
Add 1 package frozen chopped spinach, thawed and squeezed dry, to the onion and garlic mixture and sauté for a few minutes (until the moisture has evaporated) before adding the flour.

Bean Con Queso Dip
Stir a 14 oz (398 mL) can of mashed kidney beans or refried beans into the dip, and use a full 8 oz package of cream cheese.

Contents per serving

Calories	94
Total fat	5.6 g
saturated fat	3.1 g
monounsaturated fat	2.0 g
polyunsaturated fat	0.5 g
Protein	4.1 g
Carbohydrates	6.8 g
Cholesterol	16.0 mg
Fiber	1.3 g
Calories from fat	55%

Seven Layer Dip

This Seven Layer dip has closer to 9 layers, but who's counting? If you don't want to bother preparing the bean layer, substitute a can of refried beans or vegetarian chili, which is usually much lower in fat than the meaty varieties. Some people like this hot and bubbly – if this sounds like you, omit the lettuce and bake it at 350 F for about 20 minutes, until it's heated through.

1 - 14 oz (398 mL) can kidney beans, rinsed and drained

1 clove garlic, crushed

1 Tbsp lime juice

1/2 tsp each chili powder

1/2 tsp ground cumin

pinch salt

2 ripe tomatoes, diced

1/2 cup salsa

1 small red, green or yellow bell pepper, seeded and diced

1 ripe avocado, peeled, pitted and mashed, OR 1 batch guacamole (see page 60)

1 Tbsp taco seasoning (optional)

1 - 8 oz (250 mL) container low fat sour cream

1 small purple onion, finely chopped

shredded iceburg lettuce (optional)

1 cup grated old cheddar cheese

1/2 cup sliced black olives (optional)

baked tortilla chips (see page 46)

1 Mash the beans with garlic, lime juice, chili powder, cumin and salt in a food processor or in a bowl with a fork; spread in a shallow dish or pie plate.

2 Stir the taco seasoning into the sour cream.

3 Layer the remaining ingredients on top of the beans in any order you like.

4 Serve immediately, or cover and chill until you're ready for it.

Serves 6.

Contents per serving

Calories	198
Total fat	9.0 g
saturated fat	3.4 g
monounsaturated fat	4.5 g
polyunsaturated fat	1.1 g
Protein	8.5 g
Carbohydrates	21.5 g
Cholesterol	13 mg
Fiber	2.2 g
Calories from fat	42%

Cheesy Black Bean Dip

My Dad is always extolling the virtues of beans, and pushing everyone to eat more of them. Being a gastroenterologist I guess he knows what he's talking about. Legumes are quite possibly the perfect food. Pound for pound they contain as much protein as steak! They are rich in soluble fiber (the best kind – and only 2 Tbsp of kidney beans gives you four times as much as 1 slice of whole wheat bread!), are an excellent source of folic acid, calcium, iron, copper, phosphorus, potassium, magnesium and zinc, and are low in fat and calories. On top of that they are dirt cheap and can be stored for longer than nearly any other food. What else could you ask for?

1 - 14 oz. (398 mL) can black beans, rinsed and drained

1 tsp canola oil

1 small onion, finely chopped

2 cloves garlic, crushed

1 large tomato, chopped

1/2 cup salsa

1/2 tsp cumin

1/2 tsp chili powder

1 Tbsp lime juice

1 cup shredded old cheddar or Monterey Jack cheese

1/2 cup chopped fresh cilantro (optional)

1 Mash black beans with a fork until chunky.

2 Heat the oil in a non-stick skillet over medium heat and saute the onion and garlic for 3 minutes, until soft. Add the beans, tomato, salsa, cumin, and chili powder; cook for 5 more minutes, stirring often. Remove from heat and stir in lime juice, cheese and cilantro, and stir until the cheese melts.

3 Serve warm or at room temperature with tortilla chips.

Serves 8.

Black Bean & Bacon Dip
Cook 3 slices of bacon in the skillet until crisp. Crumble and set aside. Drain all but 1 Tbsp of the fat from the pan and sauté the onion and garlic in it instead of using the oil. Stir the crumbled bacon into the dip along with the lime juice, cheese and cilantro.

Contents per serving

Calories	117
Total fat	3.1 g
saturated fat	1.6 g
monounsaturated fat	1.1 g
polyunsaturated fat	0.4 g
Protein	6.9 g
Carbohydrates	15.6 g
Cholesterol	7.2 mg
Fiber	4.3 g
Calories from fat	25%

Chorizo Chipotle Dip

If you can find chicken chorizo sausage (Spolumbo's makes it!) it has about a quarter the fat of regular chorizo sausage. The nutritional analysis is based on regular chorizo.

1 tsp olive or canola oil

1 spicy chorizo sausage,
finely chopped or crumbled

1 onion, finely chopped

1 red bell pepper, cored, seeded
and chopped

1-2 cloves garlic, crushed

1/2 tsp cumin

1/2 tsp oregano

1 - 19 oz (540 mL) can pinto, kidney
or navy beans, undrained

1 canned chipotle chile en adobo,
finely chopped

1/2 cup low fat sour cream

salt to taste

1 Heat the oil in a large non-stick skillet. Squeeze the chorizo sausage out of its casing into the skillet - crumbling it up - and cook over medium heat until it's no longer pink. Transfer to a small bowl.

2 If there is too much fat in the pan, drain most of it off, but there shouldn't be much. Sauté the onion, pepper and garlic in the pan until tender. Add the cumin and oregano, cook for another minute and then add the beans and chipotle pepper. Bring to a simmer, then reduce the heat and cook for about 5 minutes, stirring often.

3 Transfer the bean mixture to a food processor and pulse until it's chunky. Stir in the sausage, sour cream and salt to taste.

4 Transfer to a serving bowl and garnish with fresh cilantro if you like.

Serves 6.

Contents per serving

Calories	203
Total fat	4.8 g
saturated fat	1.9 g
monounsaturated fat	1.7 g
polyunsaturated fat	1.2 g
Protein	11.9 g
Carbohydrates	28.8 g
Cholesterol	13.3 mg
Fiber	0.6 g
Calories from fat	22%

Creamy Chicken & Charred Corn Dip

I love using leftover roast chicken, which has a lot of flavor, in dishes like this. If you don't have leftovers, sauté a finely chopped chicken breast with the onion and garlic. This is perfect to serve with tortilla chips. Rolled up in a flour tortilla, it makes an easy meal.

1 tsp olive or canola oil

1 large onion, chopped

2 cloves garlic, crushed

1 small red bell pepper, seeded and chopped

1 - 14 oz can kernel corn, drained

1 cup leftover cooked chicken, shredded or chopped

1 Tbsp chili powder

1/2 tsp cumin

salt to taste

1/2 - 8 oz (250 g) package light cream cheese

1/4 cup water or chicken stock

1 cup low fat sour cream

1/4 cup chopped fresh cilantro

1 Heat oil in a large skillet and sauté onion and garlic over medium heat until soft. Add the peppers and corn and cook until the vegetables are tender and corn is slightly charred. Add the chicken, chili powder, cumin and salt.

2 Reduce heat to low and add the cream cheese and water; stir until the cheese is melted and everything is well blended. Remove from heat and stir in the sour cream and cilantro.

Serves 8.

Contents per serving

Calories	173
Total fat	5.5 g
saturated fat	2.8 g
monounsaturated fat	2.0 g
polyunsaturated fat	0.7 g
Protein	14.3 g
Carbohydrates	16.2 g
Cholesterol	38.0 mg
Fiber	2.3 g
Calories from fat	32%

Guacamole

A simple guacamole is nothing more than avocados mashed with garlic and lime, but it lends itself well to all kinds of additions. Try stirring in $1/2$ cup salsa or sour cream, a head of roasted garlic or a handful of chopped cooked shrimp. Because avocados are very high in fat – about 75% of calories come from fat – guacamole is fairly high in calories as well. But take heart, it's virtually all healthy monounsaturated fat, the kind you want to include in your diet.

2 ripe avocados, peeled and pitted

2 Tbsp finely chopped or grated purple or white onion

1 clove garlic, crushed

juice of 1 lime

salt to taste

$1/4$ tsp ground cumin (optional)

1 tomato, seeded and chopped (optional)

2 Tbsp chopped fresh cilantro (optional)

1 Mash everything except the tomato together with a fork to make it as smooth or as chunky as you like. Stir in the tomato and cilantro if you're using it.

Serves 6.

Guacamole with Pears, Grapes & Pomegranate

I stumbled upon this fantastic combo on *gourmet.com*, and it got such rave reviews I had to try it! Omit the garlic, cumin, tomato and cilantro, and stir in 1 small peeled and chopped pear, $1/2$ cup halved seedless grapes, $1/2$ cup pomegranate seeds and 1 or 2 serrano chiles, seeded and finely chopped.

Hint
Make sure your avocados are ripe or they won't mash very well. The best way to tell if an avocado is ripe is by squeezing it - a ripe avocado will yield to gentle pressure. If you need to ripen avocados fast, put them in a paper bag with an apple to speed up the process.

Contents per serving

Calories	111
Total fat	9.3 g
saturated fat	1.6 g
monounsaturated fat	6.4 g
polyunsaturated fat	1.3 g
Protein	1.4 g
Carbohydrates	5.8 g
Cholesterol	0.0 mg
Fiber	1.8 g
Calories from fat	76%

Clockwise from bottom:
Sweet Spiced Pecans
Trail Mix
Party Mix
Granola
Maple Pecan Popcorn

Clockwise from left:
Pork Satay with Peanut Sauce (middle)
Vietnamese Rice Paper Rolls
Vietnamese Pork Meatballs
Baked Spring Rolls

Clockwise from bottom left:
Romesco Dip
Flaxseed Wafers
Lettuce Wraps with Figs, Roasted Red Peppers
   and Parmesan (in the Quickies section)
Chicken Negimaki with Sweet Red Pepper Dip
Chicken Satay

Edamamole

My sister gave me this recipe which uses edamame (soybeans) and the broccoli stalks I usually toss out in place of some of the avocado in traditional guacamole. This is a great way to cut back the calorie content. The edamame (you can find them at Asian grocery stores) also contribute protein and valuable antioxidants. Scoop away!

1/2 cup fresh or frozen edamame, out of the pods

2 broccoli stalks, peeled

1/2 small purple onion or 2 green onions, chopped

1 clove garlic, crushed

1 small jalapeño, seeded and chopped

1 - 2 ripe avocados, peeled and pitted

juice of 1 lime

salt to taste

1 tomato, chopped (optional)

2 Tbsp chopped fresh cilantro (optional)

1 Bring a saucepan of salted water to a boil and cook the edamame and broccoli for a few minutes, until very tender. Run cold water over them and drain well.

2 Put the edamame and broccoli in the bowl of a food processor with the onion, garlic and jalapeno and process until finely chopped. Add the avocado, lime juice and salt and pulse until smooth, scraping down the sides of the bowl. Transfer to a bowl and stir in the tomato and cilantro, if you're using it.

Makes about 2 cups. Serves 6.

Contents per serving

Calories	94
Total fat	6.0 g
saturated fat	1.0 g
monounsaturated fat	3.5 g
polyunsaturated fat	1.5 g
Protein	4.3 g
Carbohydrates	7.0 g
Cholesterol	0.0 mg
Fiber	2.8 g
Calories from fat	57%

Classic Tomato Salsa

Salsas have hardly any calories but are packed with antioxidants (especially carotenoids like beta-carotene and lycopene), vitamins C and E and potassium. Try cutting the tomatoes in half and roasting them first under the broiler until they're blackened, then pulsing everything in a food processor. Roasting adds a smoky flavor.

3 ripe tomatoes, finely chopped

1 clove garlic, crushed

3 Tbsp finely chopped purple onion

1 Tbsp lime juice

1 jalapeño pepper, seeded and minced (or more if you like it hot!)

2 Tbsp chopped fresh cilantro or basil

salt to taste

1 Stir everything together in a bowl. Makes about 2^{1}/2 cups.

Avocado Salsa
Stir a chopped ripe avocado into the salsa.

Contents per ^{1}/2 cup

Calories	21
Total fat	0.1 g
saturated fat	0.0 g
monounsaturated fat	0.0 g
polyunsaturated fat	0.1 g
Protein	0.8 g
Carbohydrates	4.7 g
Cholesterol	0.0 mg
Fiber	1.0 g
Calories from fat	11%

Olive & Basil Salsa

Make sure you choose ripe, flavorful tomatoes – it will make all the difference in your salsas.

4 ripe tomatoes, finely chopped

1/4 - 1/2 cup fresh basil, torn up or chopped

1/4 cup sliced Kalamata olives

1 Tbsp capers (optional)

1 Tbsp olive oil

1/2 tsp sugar

salt and freshly ground pepper to taste

1 Stir everything together in a bowl.

Makes about 3 cups.

Contents per 1/2 cup

Calories	46
Total fat	3.2 g
saturated fat	0.5 g
monounsaturated fat	2.3 g
polyunsaturated fat	0.4 g
Protein	0.8 g
Carbohydrates	4.2 g
Cholesterol	0.0 mg
Fiber	1.3 g
Calories from fat	60%

Black Bean & Mango Salsa

Sweet, juicy mango is rich in vitamins A and C and makes a delicious contrast to protein-packed black beans. To dice the mango, slice it lengthwise along the flat seed to remove both 'cheeks', score them without cutting through the skin, then flip it inside out and cut the flesh off the skin.

1 - 19 oz (540 mL) can black beans, rinsed and drained

1 mango, peeled and chopped

1/4 cup finely chopped red onion

2 Tbsp chopped fresh cilantro

1 finely chopped jalapeño pepper and/or canned chipotle chile in adobo sauce

a few drops Tabasco sauce

salt to taste

1 Stir everything together in a bowl.

Makes about 2 1/2 cups.

Contents per 1/2 cup

Calories	174
Total fat	0.6 g
saturated fat	0.2 g
monounsaturated fat	0.1 g
polyunsaturated fat	0.3 g
Protein	9.9 g
Carbohydrates	33.7 g
Cholesterol	0.0 mg
Fiber	8.5 g
Calories from fat	4%

Pico de Gallo

Sometimes it's hard to find nice tomatoes at the market, but it's always easy to get your hands on a can of them. Use a large (28 oz) can and omit the fresh tomatoes if you want. I make mine with Muir Glen fire-roasted tomatoes.

3 ripe tomatoes, finely chopped

1 - 14 oz (398 mL) can diced tomatoes, drained

1 purple or white onion, finely chopped

2 fresh jalapeno peppers, seeded and minced, or more to taste

1/2 bunch fresh cilantro

juice of 1 lime (or 2 Tbsp)

2 cloves garlic, crushed

1 Tbsp sugar

1/2 tsp ground cumin

1/2 tsp salt

1 Tbsp olive oil (optional)

1. Stir everything together in a large bowl, crushing the tomatoes if they are too chunky. Drain off some of the juice if it is too watery. If you want to use a food processor, pulse the onion, garlic and peppers first until finely chopped. Add everything else and pulse once or twice, until blended but still chunky.

Makes about 3 cups.

Contents per 1/2 cup

Calories	44
Total fat	0.4 g
saturated fat	0.1 g
monounsaturated fat	0.1 g
polyunsaturated fat	0.2 g
Protein	1.4 g
Carbohydrates	10.1 g
Cholesterol	0.0 mg
Fiber	1.8 g
Calories from fat	9%

Curried Shrimp Chutney Dip

Everyone goes nuts for this dip, and it takes about 5 minutes to stir together. It's one of those recipes that produces spectacular results with minimal effort. And it's equally delicious made with crab or with a combination of shrimp and crab.

1/2 - 8 oz (250 g) tub light cream cheese

1/2 cup light sour cream

2 green onions, finely chopped

1/4 cup finely chopped red pepper
or roasted red pepper

1/3 cup mango or peach chutney

1 clove garlic, crushed

1 tsp curry powder or paste,
or more to taste

salt and pepper to taste

1 lb cooked shrimp, chopped,
or cocktail-size shrimp

1. Combine the cream cheese and sour cream in a medium bowl and beat until smooth. Stir in green onions, red pepper, chutney, garlic, curry powder, salt, pepper and shrimp. Spoon into a bowl and chill.

2. Serve with fresh naan torn into pieces, veggies, pita or bagel chips.

Serves 6.

Contents per serving

Calories	195
Total fat	5.3 g
saturated fat	3.0 g
monounsaturated fat	1.6 g
polyunsaturated fat	0.7 g
Protein	18.7 g
Carbohydrates	16.6 g
Cholesterol	130 mg
Fiber	0.7 g
Calories from fat	28%

Hummus

There are so many ways to make hummus, and it is one of the fastest snacks around. You can whiz up a batch of it in under 5 minutes in the food processor. I love eating it for lunch at my desk with a fresh pita to tear and dip, and it makes a great TV or movie snack instead of popcorn or chips. If you don't have tahini, peanut butter makes a delicious substitute. If you miss the sesame flavor tahini gives your hummus, a drizzle of sesame oil will do the trick.

1 - 19 oz (540 mL) can chickpeas (garbanzo beans), rinsed and drained

2 Tbsp light peanut butter or tahini (sesame seed paste)

2 Tbsp plain yogurt

2 cloves garlic, peeled

1 Tbsp olive oil (optional)

juice of 1 lemon

1/2 tsp cumin (optional)

salt and pepper to taste

1 Place garlic in a food processor and process to finely chop. Add everything else but the salt and pepper and whiz, scraping down the sides of the bowl, until you have a nice thick puree. Add salt and pepper to taste, and a little water if it's too thick.

2 Serve with toasted pita chips and fresh veggies to dip with or spread on a pita or tortilla and fill with grilled chicken and/or roasted veggies to make a wrap.

Makes about 2 cups.

Contents per 1/3 cup

Calories	99
Total fat	2.7 g
saturated fat	0.5 g
monounsaturated fat	1.1 g
polyunsaturated fat	1.1 g
Protein	5.8 g
Carbohydrates	14.3 g
Cholesterol	0.3 mg
Fiber	2.0 g
Calories from fat	25%

Hummus Variations

There are lots of ways to jazz up your hummus. Here are a few ideas.

Roasted Red Pepper Hummus
Whiz in 2 roasted red peppers, and be sure to include the cumin. For Chipotle Red Pepper Hummus, add 1 Tbsp of minced canned chipotle chilies as well. Adds virtually no fat or calories, but plenty of vitamins A and C!

Mediterranean Hummus
Once hummus is blended and smooth, stir in 1/2 cup sliced Kalamata olives, 1/4 cup crumbled feta, and a 6 oz jar of artichoke hearts, drained and finely chopped. Or whiz in a roasted red pepper, a few crushed olives, 1/3 cup fresh parsley and 1 Tbsp of hot sauce. Adds about 55 calories and just under 4 grams of fat per serving for the olive-feta version.

Spicy Hummus
Add 1 tsp each ground cumin & coriander and 1/2 tsp crushed red pepper flakes or a shot of hot pepper sauce.

Balsamic Onion Hummus
Saute 1 large chopped onion in 1 tsp oil for 10 minutes, until golden. Add 2 Tbsp balsamic vinegar and cook until vinegar evaporates; cool. Add to the hummus and top with 1 Tbsp chopped fresh cilantro.

Pumpkin Hummus
Add a small can of pumpkin puree to the mixture, and include the cumin. Canned pumpkin adds a hefty boost of beta carotene – 20 times more than fresh!

Roasted Garlic Hummus
Substitute 1 head of roasted garlic for the fresh garlic.

Roasted Garlic Edamame Hummus
Substitute 1 1/2 cups cooked edamame (soybeans), or one can of soybeans for the chickpeas, and replace fresh garlic with one head of roasted garlic. Top with chopped fresh cilantro.

Roasted Carrot Hummus
Cut about a pound of carrots into chunks, toss with oil and roast, covered with foil, for about half an hour. Remove the foil and roast for another 20 minutes. Add to the chickpea mixture and puree. Use twice the amount of peanut butter. Adds about 50 calories and 2 grams of fat per serving.

Fresh Pea Hummus
Replace the chick peas with 2 cups shelled peas, boiled until tender. Add a small handful of chopped fresh cilantro as well.

Roasted Garlic & White Bean Spread

At the risk of repeating myself, beans are the most concentrated food source of natural fiber, and are packed with protein, essential vitamins and minerals. A small container of bean spread with a baggie of crackers or veggies makes a great portable snack. If you want to kick up the flavor, add a few shots of Tabasco.

1 large head garlic

1 - 19 oz (540 mL) can white kidney beans, rinsed and drained

1 Tbsp olive oil

1 Tbsp lemon juice

pinch salt

1 Tbsp chopped fresh rosemary or sage (optional)

Contents per serving

Calories	68
Total fat	1.9 g
saturated fat	0.3 g
monounsaturated fat	1.3 g
polyunsaturated fat	0.3 g
Protein	3.3 g
Carbohydrates	10.0 g
Cholesterol	0 mg
Fiber	2.3 g
Calories from fat	21%

1 Cut a thin slice off the top of the head of garlic and wrap the head in foil. Bake it at 350 F for about an hour, until the garlic is soft. You can do several heads at a time, or throw a bulb or two in the oven when you're baking something else. Store the roasted garlic in the fridge until you're ready for it.

2 In the bowl of a food processor combine the beans, olive oil, lemon juice, salt and rosemary. Squeeze in the roasted cloves of garlic. Pulse a few times to combine the ingredients – process it completely if you want a smooth dip, or leave it chunky. Serve with crostini, pita chips, breadsticks, crackers or veggies.

Serves 8.

Baked White Bean Spread

Sauté 1 chopped onion in 1 tsp canola oil until pale golden, and stir into the finished dip. Spread in an ovenproof dish and sprinkle with grated Parmesan cheese or swirl in a few spoonfuls of goat cheese. Bake at 350 F for 20 - 30 minutes, until bubbly.

White Bean & Roasted Pepper Spread

Add 1 roasted red pepper (see page 73) and 1/2 cup chopped fresh basil, and process as directed.

Italian White Bean Spread

Stir 1/2 cup each finely chopped onion and roasted red pepper into the dip, along with a drizzle of Italian dressing and 1/4 cup chopped fresh parsley. Spread in an ovenproof dish and sprinkle with grated parmesan cheese. Bake at 350 F for 20 - 30 minutes, until bubbly.

Yogurt & Feta White Bean Spread

Add 1 cup plain yogurt and 1/2 cup crumbled feta cheese and blend as directed. Stir in 1 chopped green onion or sprinkle it over top.

White Bean Guacamole

Stir 1 mashed ripe avocado into the bean mixture, and use lime juice instead of lemon. Stir in 1 chopped tomato and 2 Tbsp chopped fresh cilantro.

Tzatziki

Regular yogurt, preferably thick Greek yogurt, is far superior to the runny low-fat or fat-free varieties that are most commonly found at the grocery store. Even 'full-fat' yogurts generally only contain about 3 grams per 1/2 cup, and it's much more delicious and satisfying.

1 small cucumber, peeled if necessary

1 - 2 cloves garlic, crushed

2 cups good quality plain yogurt, preferably Balkan-style

salt and pepper to taste

1. Grate the cucumber with a box grater onto a double thickness of paper towel. Gather up the cucumber in the towel and squeeze out as much excess water as you can.

2. Combine cucumber, garlic, yogurt, salt and pepper in a bowl and stir until well blended. If you like, add a squeeze of lemon. The garlic flavor will intensify the longer it sits.

Makes about 2 1/2 - 3 cups.

Contents per 1/3 cup

Calories	45
Total fat	1.0 g
saturated fat	0.6 g
monounsaturated fat	0.3 g
polyunsaturated fat	0.1 g
Protein	3.5 g
Carbohydrates	5.6 g
Cholesterol	3.7 mg
Fiber	0.3 g
Calories from fat	20%

Artichoke Tzatziki Dip

My testers adored this dip and everyone asked for the recipe. It's really fast and easy, especially if you cheat and use store bought tzatziki and bottled roasted red peppers.

2 cups tzatziki, homemade or store-bought

1/2 cup Kalamata olives, pitted and chopped

2 red peppers, roasted and chopped (page 73)

1 - 6 oz (170mL) jar marinated artichoke hearts, drained and chopped

4 roma tomatoes, seeded and chopped

3 green onions, chopped

1. Stir the olives, peppers, artichokes, tomatoes and green onions into the tzatziki dip. Serve with fresh pitas or pita chips.

   Serves 8.

Contents per serving

Calories	94
Total fat	2.2 g
saturated fat	0.8 g
monounsaturated fat	1.1 g
polyunsaturated fat	0.3 g
Protein	5.5 g
Carbohydrates	14.6 g
Cholesterol	3.7 mg
Fiber	3.4 g
Calories from fat	22%

Baba Ghanouj

Baba Ghanouj (pronounced ganoosh) is a Middle Eastern dip made with roasted eggplant. If you're having a party, this is perfect served with hummus, roasted red pepper dip and a big bowl of pita chips. Be warned – you will have garlic breath.

2 medium eggplants

1/4 cup tahini (sesame seed paste)

2 cloves garlic, crushed

2 Tbsp lemon juice

1 tsp salt, or to taste

drizzle of olive oil (optional)

Contents per serving

Calories	74
Total fat	3.6 g
saturated fat	0.5 g
monounsaturated fat	1.4 g
polyunsaturated fat	1.7 g
Protein	2.5 g
Carbohydrates	9.4 g
Cholesterol	0.0 mg
Fiber	0.7 g
Calories from fat	42%

1. Preheat oven to 475 F.

2. Place whole eggplants on a baking dish and roast, turning once or twice, for 45 minutes to an hour, until skin is charred and eggplant is soft. Set aside until cool enough to handle.

3. Scoop the flesh out of the eggplant and roughly mash with a fork. Stir in tahini, garlic, lemon juice and salt. Leave it coarse or whiz it in the food processor until it is as smooth as you like. If necessary, thin with a little extra lemon juice or water.

4. Transfer to a bowl and drizzle with olive oil. Serve with pita chips, veggies or grilled bread.

Serves 8.

Creamy Baba Ghanouj
Add a few big spoonfuls of plain (preferably Balkan-style) yogurt in the food processor.

Roasted Eggplant & Tomato Dip
Mash the roasted eggplant coarsely with a fork. Omit tahini and lemon juice and stir in 1 chopped tomato, 1/4 cup finely chopped purple onion and 1 Tbsp balsamic vinegar. Top with chopped cilantro or Italian parsley.

Roasted Red Pepper & Garlic Dip

This dip is amazingly creamy considering how little fat it contains. Its flavor and texture reminds me of something cheesy.

2 red bell peppers

1 head garlic

1/2 cup light sour cream

1 Tbsp olive oil (optional)

1/2 tsp ground cumin

1/2 tsp salt, or to taste

pinch cayenne (optional)

Contents per serving

Calories	78
Total fat	1.5 g
saturated fat	0.9 g
monounsaturated fat	0.4 g
polyunsaturated fat	0.2 g
Protein	3.3 g
Carbohydrates	13.4 g
Cholesterol	5.0 mg
Fiber	1.5 g
Calories from fat	19%

1. Preheat oven to 475 F.

2. Cut peppers in half lengthwise, clean out the ribs and seeds and place them cut-side-down on a baking sheet lined with foil. Separate the garlic cloves, leaving the skins intact, and wrap together in a piece of foil. Place on the baking sheet with the peppers and roast both until the pepper skins have blackened.

3. Remove from the oven and place the peppers in a bowl; cover with plastic wrap, foil or a tea towel and set aside to cool. This will give them a chance to steam. Let the garlic cool in its foil too.

4. When they are cool enough to handle, peel the skins off the peppers and remove the seeds, and place them into the bowl of a food processor. Pour in the juices that have collected in the bottom of the bowl and squeeze the garlic cloves out of their papery skins into the bowl.

5. Add the sour cream, olive oil, cumin, salt and cayenne and blend until smooth. Transfer to a bowl and serve, or chill for up to 4 days before serving with veggies, pitas or tortilla chips.

Makes about 1 1/2 cups. Serves 4.

Roasted Red Pepper and Feta Dip

This is a surprisingly rich dip, and one that everyone seems to love. If you want to cut back the calories even further, use half the amount of feta – a little goes a long way! This dip gets 60% of its calories from fat – this is because red peppers are extremely low in calories, so most of the calories come from the cheese and oil, even though the peppers bulk it up quite a bit. If you want, you can use light feta cheese to cut back the fat even further. Note that half the fat is the healthy, unsaturated kind!

3 red bell peppers, roasted,
or a jar of roasted red peppers

1/2 cup crumbled feta cheese (about 100 g)

1 Tbsp olive oil

2 Tbsp pine nuts (optional)

Contents per serving

Calories	87
Total fat	5.8 g
saturated fat	2.9 g
monounsaturated fat	2.5 g
polyunsaturated fat	0.4 g
Protein	3.2 g
Carbohydrates	6.0 g
Cholesterol	15.3 mg
Fiber	1.2 g
Calories from fat	60%

1. To roast the peppers, leave them whole or cut them lengthwise in half and remove the ribs and seeds. Place cut side down on a baking sheet and broil until the skins have blackened. (If you are roasting them whole, turn them over halfway through so they blacken all over.) Transfer the peppers to a bowl, cover with a tea towel, plate or tin foil and let them sit until they are cool enough to handle. This will allow them to steam and the skins will slip right off. Peel the skins off with your fingers but no matter what you do, don't run them under water – that washes the flavor away! Voila – roasted peppers.

2. Put everything in a food processor and puree until smooth. Spoon into a bowl and chill for at least an hour to allow the flavors to blend. Serve with pita chips or veggies.

Serves 6.

Feta Chili Dip
Replace the red peppers with roasted Anaheim or poblano chilis, or add 1 small red chili, seeded and finely chopped, or 1 canned chili en abodo to the mixture.

Olive Tapenade

A tapenade is a condiment from the Provence region of France typically made with olives, capers, and other seasonings. Although this version does contain less fat than traditional recipes, it's still pretty high in fat. It is important to note that it is virtually all healthy monounsaturated fat, the kind we need to include more of in our diets! And because it's so pungently flavored you only need a teeny bit of it. Olive tapenade makes an excellent alternative to mayo on roasted chicken or veggie sandwiches, and is awesome tossed with hot pasta, roasted tomatoes and crumbled feta cheese. And a jar of it keeps for a long time in the fridge.

1 cup pitted Kalamata olives or other good quality brine-cured black olives

3 cloves garlic, peeled

2 - 4 anchovy fillets, or a good squeeze of anchovy paste (optional)

1 - 2 Tbsp capers, drained

1 tsp chopped fresh thyme (optional)

1 tsp chopped fresh rosemary

1 Tbsp lemon juice

1/4 cup extra virgin olive oil

1 Place garlic, olives, anchovies, capers, thyme, rosemary and lemon juice in the bowl of a food processor and pulse to chop and blend. With the motor running, slowly drizzle the olive oil through the feed tube and process until pureed. Add a pinch of pepper if you like, but because the olives, anchovies and capers are so salty, it won't need additional salt.

2 Serve with crackers or fresh breadsticks.

Serves 8.

Contents per serving

Calories	86
Total fat	8.8 g
saturated fat	1.3 g
monounsaturated fat	6.7 g
polyunsaturated fat	0.8 g
Protein	0.6 g
Carbohydrates	0.8 g
Cholesterol	0.8 mg
Fiber	0.8 g
Calories from fat	94%

Olive & Sun-dried Tomato Tapenade
Replace 1/2 cup olives with chopped sun dried tomatoes and add a roasted red pepper. Process as directed. This is good with fresh basil instead of rosemary.

Mushroom Tapenade
Sauté 2 - 3 cups chopped mushrooms (button, cremini, shiitake or Portobello) in half the oil until golden and liquid has evaporated. Add it to the olive mixture and cut the amount of olives in half.

Antipasto

Every year my sisters and I make antipasto at Christmas time, and eat so much we are sick of it until next Christmas. I think the best part about antipasto is the fun we have in the kitchen chopping and stirring the giant pot. Antipasto requires a lot of chopping – it really can't be done in the food processor or the texture turns to mush – but besides that it is really quite easy. This recipe will make a batch large enough to keep you in antipasto for a long time, with enough extra jars to give away. If you can't bear to share, extras freeze very well.

1/2 cup olive or canola oil, or use half of each

1 small head cauliflower, separated into small flowerets

2 purple onions, chopped

2 - 375 mL cans or jars pitted black olives, sliced

2 - 375 mL cans or jars manzanilla olives, sliced

2 small green peppers, chopped (or use red or yellow if you like)

3 - 106 g cans small shrimp, drained, or about 300g cooked shrimp, chopped

3 - 184 g cans tuna in water, drained

3³/4 cups (about 60 oz) ketchup

1 cup white vinegar

2 - 10 oz (284 mL) cans sliced mushrooms, drained

1 In a large stock pot, combine oil, cauliflower, onions and olives and bring to a boil over medium-high heat. Cook, stirring often, for 5 minutes.

2 Add the remaining ingredients and heat to almost boiling. If you are using jars, pour the hot antipasto into sterilized jars, seal and cool. Otherwise cool the antipasto in the pot and then transfer to plastic containers and store in the refrigerator or freeze.

3 Serve with crackers.

Makes about 12 cups.

Contents per 1/4 cup

Calories	76
Total fat	3.5 g
saturated fat	0.5 g
monounsaturated fat	2.6 g
polyunsaturated fat	0.4 g
Protein	3.6 g
Carbohydrates	8.3 g
Cholesterol	8.7 mg
Fiber	1.2 g
Calories from fat	42%

Radish & Roasted Red Pepper Dip

Peppery radishes are usually destined to be a garnish, and overlooked as a main ingredient. This is a fantastic dip to serve with veggies.

1/2 - 8 oz (250 g) package light cream cheese

1/2 cup low fat sour cream

12 large radishes

2 red bell peppers, roasted (see page 73) and finely chopped

small handful of chives, chopped

salt & pepper to taste

1. In a medium bowl, beat the cream cheese and sour cream until smooth.

2. Wash and coarsely grate the radishes. Add them to the cream cheese mixture along with the red peppers, chives, salt and pepper. Stir well.

3. Refrigerate for a few hours to allow the flavors to blend. Serve with fresh veggies.

Serves about 8.

Contents per serving

Calories	73
Total fat	3.4 g
saturated fat	2.1 g
monounsaturated fat	1.1 g
polyunsaturated fat	0.2 g
Protein	3.0 g
Carbohydrates	7.5 g
Cholesterol	11.4 mg
Fiber	2.2 g
Calories from fat	46%

Buttermilk Peppercorn Dip

This is a fresh-tasting and simple dip to serve with crudités – much better than buying a packet of mix.

1 cup low fat sour cream

$^1/_2$ cup buttermilk

1 large shallot, grated or minced

1 tsp freshly ground black pepper

$^1/_2$ tsp salt

1 Stir together all the ingredients until smooth. Serve with fresh veggies.

Makes about 1$^1/_2$ cups.

Contents per 2 Tbsp

Calories	29
Total fat	1.0 g
saturated fat	0.6 g
monounsaturated fat	0.3 g
polyunsaturated fat	0.1 g
Protein	1.4 g
Carbohydrates	3.5 g
Cholesterol	3.5 mg
Fiber	0.1 g
Calories from fat	33%

Curried Veggie Dip

This is great to make ahead (it tastes better the next day anyway) and keep in the fridge with some cut-up veggies for snacking. It's much easier to snack on veggies and dip when you don't have to prep them first!

$^1/_2$ cup low fat sour cream

$^1/_2$ cup light mayonnaise

1 tsp lemon juice, or to taste

1 tsp curry powder

$^1/_2$ tsp cumin

$^1/_4$ tsp turmeric

$^1/_4$ tsp salt

1 green onion, finely chopped

1 Whisk together all the ingredients. Serve with fresh veggies.

Makes about 1$^1/_2$ cups.

Contents per 2 Tbsp

Calories	41
Total fat	2.8 g
saturated fat	0.4 g
monounsaturated fat	1.6 g
polyunsaturated fat	0.8 g
Protein	0.6 g
Carbohydrates	3.0 g
Cholesterol	1.7 mg
Fiber	0.1 g
Calories from fat	65%

Romesco Dip

You have to try this dip – the first time I did I was instantly addicted! I adore it. The toasted almonds and bread thickens the dip and adds depth to the flavor and body to the texture. I often make a batch on Sundays to keep in the fridge and dip into with a spoon all week. All the fat comes from the almonds and olive oil, making this a great source of healthy monounsaturated fat.

¼ cup sliced or slivered almonds, or half almonds and half pine nuts

1 clove garlic, peeled

2 thick slices French bread, toasted

2 red peppers, roasted (see page 73)

1 Tbsp red wine, sherry or balsamic vinegar

½ tsp paprika

¼ tsp chili flakes

2 Tbsp olive oil

Contents per ¼ cup

Calories	167
Total fat	10.3 g
saturated fat	1.4 g
monounsaturated fat	8.1 g
polyunsaturated fat	0.8 g
Protein	3.5 g
Carbohydrates	13.4 g
Cholesterol	0.0 mg
Fiber	2.2 g
Calories from fat	61%

1 Toast almonds and garlic in a small, dry saucepan over medium heat for about 3 minutes, until the almonds are pale golden and fragrant. Transfer to a food processor. Tear the bread into chunks into the food processor. Pulse until the bread and nuts turn to crumbs.

2 Add the red peppers, vinegar, paprika and chili flakes and whiz until well blended. With the motor running, slowly drizzle in the olive oil and process until the mixture has the consistency of thick mayonnaise, scraping down the sides of the bowl.

3 Use to dip cooked, chilled tail-on shrimp, grilled bread or veggies.

Makes 1 cup.

Muhammara

I am absolutely hooked on the Muhammara – a Middle Eastern dip made with walnuts, red peppers and pomegranate – at Aida's on Fourth Street in Calgary. My not-so-subtle pleas for the recipe have been futile – apparently I'm not the only one who's asked! So I did a little research and came up with my own version. Virtually all of the fat in Muhammara is healthy mono- and poly-unsaturated. Pomegranate molasses can be found at gourmet and ethnic grocery stores and is well worth the effort to find.

3 red bell peppers, roasted (see page 73)

1 small hot red pepper, roasted along with the bell peppers (optional)

1/2 cup fresh bread crumbs

1/2 cup walnuts, toasted and finely chopped

2 cloves garlic, crushed

1 Tbsp lemon juice

1 Tbsp pomegranate molasses

1/4 tsp cumin (optional)

1 - 2 Tbsp olive oil

1 In the bowl of a food processor, pulse the roasted peppers, bread crumbs, walnuts, garlic, lemon juice, pomegranate molasses and cumin until well blended and smooth.

2 With the motor running, slowly pour the olive oil through the feed tube until the mixture is smooth and creamy. If it's too thick, add a few spoonfuls of water. To serve, spread the muhammara in a bowl, top with a walnut half and drizzle with a little extra olive oil if you like. Serve with fresh pitas or pita chips.

Makes about 1¹/2 cups.

Contents per ¹/4 cup

Calories	164
Total fat	8.8 g
saturated fat	0.8 g
monounsaturated fat	3.2 g
polyunsaturated fat	4.3 g
Protein	4.7 g
Carbohydrates	19 g
Cholesterol	0.0 mg
Fiber	2.2 g
Calories from fat	45%

Fruit Dips

Who says only veggies need dips? A big bowl of fruit served with fruit dip is always a good idea. There's something celebratory about being able to dunk your food into something yummy. Maybe that's why kids like it so much. For a great summertime snack or dessert, thread chunks of fresh pineapple, apple, banana, peaches, strawberries and mango on bamboo skewers to make fruit kabobs and serve alongside any of these dips. If you like, quickly grill them on a well-oiled BBQ first. Cubes of pound cake go really well between the fruit too.

Creamy Fruit Dip
Fold together equal parts fruit flavored yogurt and Cool Whip Light.

Strawberry Fruit Dip
Blend 1 package frozen, thawed strawberries in a food processor or blender until smooth. Stir into the yogurt mixture.

Sour Cream with Brown Sugar
Stir a few Tbsp of brown sugar into 1 - 2 cups of low-fat sour cream.

Marshmallow Peach Fruit Dip
Stir together 1/4 cup peach preserves, 1/4 cup low-fat sour cream and 1 jar of marshmallow crème.

Dulce de Leche
Pour 2 cans of low-fat sweetened condensed milk into a pie plate and cover with foil. Bake at 425 F for an hour and a half, until it's thick and golden. Stir in 1/2 tsp vanilla and a pinch of salt. For Rum Dulce de Leche, stir in 1/4 cup dark rum too.

Creamy Key Lime Dip
Stir together 1 can of low-fat sweetened condensed milk, 1 can of evaporated milk, 1/2 cup lime juice (Key lime juice if you can get it) and the zest of 1 lime. I like dipping graham crackers in this – it reminds me of the pie!

Chocolate Fondue
Melt 1/2 lb of chopped semisweet chocolate and stir it into 1 can of Hershey's chocolate syrup. This cuts the fat drastically – Hershey's chocolate syrup is virtually fat free!

Cranberry Orange Goat Cheese Schmear

The term *schmear* is thought to have come from the Yiddish word *shmirn* ("to smear or grease"), and refers to fancied-up cream cheese spreads for your bagel. Try spreading schmears on mini bagels and piling them on a platter for a party, or take some for lunch.

1 - 8 oz (250 g) tub light cream cheese

1/4 cup soft fresh goat cheese
(such as Montrachet)

2 Tbsp plain yogurt

1 Tbsp honey, or to taste

1/4 cup dried cranberries or cherries

1 tsp grated orange zest (optional)

1 Stir all the ingredients together in a bowl until smooth. Store in a container in the refrigerator.

Makes about 1 1/2 cups.

Contents per Tbsp

Calories	48
Total fat	3.3 g
saturated fat	2.2 g
monounsaturated fat	1.0 g
polyunsaturated fat	0.1 g
Protein	2.4 g
Carbohydrates	1.7 g
Cholesterol	11.0 mg
Fiber	0.1 g
Calories from fat	66%

Creamy & Spicy Tuna Schmear

This is made with those little tins of flavored tuna, which are packed in water but have tons of flavor. I usually spread this on bagels, but I've recently discovered it's great to spread on a flour tortilla, stuff with fresh veggies and roll up into a portable wrap.

1/2 - 8 oz (250 g) tub light cream cheese

2 Tbsp light mayonnaise

1 - 85 g tin flavored tuna, such as spicy Thai

1/4 cup finely chopped celery

1/4 cup finely chopped red bell pepper

salt and pepper to taste

1 In a medium bowl, beat cream cheese and mayonnaise until well blended and smooth. Stir in the tuna, celery, red pepper, salt and pepper. Serve in a bowl with bagel chips or crostini (see page 43), or spread it on bagels or tortillas.

Makes about 1 1/2 cups.

Contents per Tbsp

Calories	19
Total fat	1.2 g
saturated fat	0.6 g
monounsaturated fat	0.5 g
polyunsaturated fat	0.1 g
Protein	1.5 g
Carbohydrates	0.5 g
Cholesterol	36 mg
Fiber	0.0 g
Calories from fat	59%

Finger Lickin' Food

The best food, I think, is the kind that requires a lot of napkins and finger licking. Foods that may warrant a shower afterwards are the ones that seem to inspire equally passionate enthusiasm from the friends I share them with.

Foods that drip aren't the best choice for fancy schmancy parties, but they are perfect for any occasion at which you won't be embarrassed if you have to lick off your hands, and maybe even your arm. Kids are fans of finger foods too – crunchy chicken fingers, pizza, cheese sticks and buffalo chicken drumsticks are always well-received, especially when served restaurant-style on a big platter with some fresh veggies and dip to round out the meal. No one will realize they're eating healthier, so don't bother telling them.

Chicken Fingers with Honey Mustard

This is a fantastically versatile recipe, perfect if you don't have much in your cupboard. All you need is some chicken and any form of crunchy crumb to coat it with. If you can find Panko – extra crunchy Japanese crumbs that create a wonderful crust – grab some! If you don't want to turn on the oven, cook them in a non-stick sauté pan. Serve your chicken fingers with honey mustard or bottled plum sauce for dipping.

3 skinless, boneless chicken breast halves, cut into strips (about 1 lb)

1 large egg or 1/2 cup buttermilk

1 - 2 cups corn flake crumbs, dry breadcrumbs, finely crushed crackers or Panko (Japanese breadcrumbs)

1/4 cup grated Parmesan cheese or ground pecans

salt and pepper to taste

honey & mustard for dipping

Contents per serving

Calories	264
Total fat	4.2 g
saturated fat	2.1 g
monounsaturated fat	1.5 g
polyunsaturated fat	0.6 g
Protein	31.2 g
Carbohydrates	20.9 g
Cholesterol	124.6 mg
Fiber	0.6 g
Calories from fat	18%

1. Preheat oven to 375 F.

2. Break the egg into a shallow dish and beat it a little with a fork. If you are using buttermilk, pour it over the chicken and refrigerate for an hour. Combine crumbs, parmesan or pecans, and salt and pepper in another shallow dish.

3. Dip chicken strips into egg (or remove from buttermilk) and roll in crumbs to coat well. Place about 1" apart on a greased baking sheet. If you want, lightly spray the strips with cooking spray.

4. Bake for 15 - 20 minutes, until golden and cooked through. Mix equal amounts of honey and mustard for dipping.

Serves 4.

Curried Almond Chicken Fingers
Coat chicken strips in a mixture of 1 1/2 cups bread crumbs, 1/2 cup finely chopped almonds, and 1 tsp curry powder.

Pecan Crusted Chicken Fingers
Coat chicken strips in a mixture of 3/4 cup finely chopped pecans, 1/2 cup corn flake or Panko crumbs, 2 Tbsp flour, salt and pepper.

Spicy Chicken Fingers
Add 1 tsp chili powder to the crumb mixture, and a few drops of Tabasco sauce to the egg.

Crunchy Buffalo Chicken Fingers
Dip chicken strips in low-fat creamy ranch dressing spiked with 1 tsp of bottled hot pepper sauce, then roll in crumbs to coat.

Crispy Sesame Chicken Fingers
Roll chicken strips in a mixture of half crumbs, half sesame seeds. Serve with sweet and sour sauce.

Buffalo Drumsticks

The ultimate finger food, I think, is one that requires a lot of finger-licking. Chicken wings are the best for this, but they are all skin, which is high in fat. And the hot wing sauce typically served in restaurants is equal parts hot sauce and butter! Skinned drumsticks are even better than wings – more meat, and you can still eat them with your fingers.

8 chicken drumsticks, skinned and trimmed of any fat

1/4 cup Tabasco or other hot sauce

2 Tbsp butter, melted

1 Tbsp red wine vinegar

1/2 tsp paprika

1/2 tsp salt

1 Combine the Tabasco, butter, vinegar, paprika and salt. Add the drumsticks and toss to coat.

2 Grill or broil the drumsticks, brushing with the hot sauce mixture, for about 20 minutes or until they're cooked through.

Makes 8 drumsticks.

Contents per drumstick

Calories	100
Total fat	4.5 g
saturated fat	2.3 g
monounsaturated fat	1.5 g
polyunsaturated fat	0.7 g
Protein	12.9 g
Carbohydrates	0.3 g
Cholesterol	55.5 mg
Fiber	0.1 g
Calories from fat	46%

Sticky, Spicy Drumsticks

These are reminiscent of sweet and sour chicken, but with a spicy kick. Use less hot sauce if you're feeding kids; more if you like to live dangerously. These do the trick when I'm craving a big sticky basketful of chicken wings. Cook them under the broiler or throw them on the grill for a smokier flavor.

8 chicken drumsticks, skinned and trimmed of any fat

1/2 cup ketchup

1/4 cup honey

1/4 cup rice vinegar

2 Tbsp brown sugar

1 Tbsp soy sauce

1 Tbsp Worcestershire sauce

1 Tbsp Tabasco or other hot sauce

2 - 3 cloves garlic, crushed

1 Combine everything but the drumsticks in a medium bowl. Add the drumsticks and stir to coat.

2 Grill or broil the drumsticks, brushing with marinade, for about 20 minutes or until cooked through. If there is extra marinade, bring it to a boil in a small pot and simmer for a minute, until thoroughly cooked. Serve with the drumsticks for dipping.

Makes 8 drumsticks.

Contents per drumstick

Calories	144
Total fat	1.9 g
saturated fat	0.6 g
monounsaturated fat	0.7 g
polyunsaturated fat	0.6 g
Protein	13.3 g
Carbohydrates	18.6 g
Cholesterol	47.7 mg
Fiber	0.3 g
Calories from fat	13%

Cheese Sticks

Who isn't a fan of deep fried cheese? These are baked rather than submerged in boiling fat, but every bit as good as the ones you order in a restaurant. If you have kids around, they will love them.

1 package mozzarella cheese strings (8 cheese strings)

2 Tbsp flour (optional)

2 large egg whites, lightly beaten with a fork

1 cup dry bread crumbs, cracker crumbs, corn flake crumbs or Panko (Japanese bread crumbs)

salt and pepper to taste

spaghetti sauce, pizza sauce or salsa for dipping (about half a cup)

Contents per stick

Calories	61
Total fat	2.3 g
saturated fat	0.1 g
monounsaturated fat	0.1 g
polyunsaturated fat	0.1 g
Protein	4.4 g
Carbohydrates	5.6 g
Cholesterol	0.0 mg
Fiber	0.4 g
Calories from fat	34%

1 Place the cheese strings in the freezer at least an hour before you plan to make these – they tend to ooze less when they're nice and cold to begin with. Preheat the oven to 400 F.

2 Place the flour, egg whites and bread crumbs in three separate bowls. Season the flour with salt and pepper. Cut the cheese strings in half widthwise. Dip one cheese stick at a time into the flour to coat, then into the egg whites and then the crumbs. Dip it into the egg again, and again into the crumbs, squeezing to help them adhere. It'll be messy, but try to cover the cheese completely. Place on a cookie sheet that has been sprayed with non-stick spray. Repeat with the remaining cheese sticks.

3 Bake for 10 - 15 minutes, until golden. Serve immediately. Warm up the spaghetti sauce and serve alongside for dipping.

Makes 16 sticks.

Mini 'Toad-in-the-Hole'

Toad-in-the-Hole is a traditional British dish made by pouring Yorkshire pudding batter over pork sausages and baking until the batter rises up crisp and crunchy around the sausage. These are bite-sized, so you're guaranteed some sausage and some Yorkie in each bite, and unlike traditional toad-in-the-hole they're remarkably low in fat. These are as good at midnight as they are at breakfast.

6 small or 3 large chicken sausages (about 170 g)

½ cup flour

½ cup milk

1 large egg

salt and pepper to taste

grainy mustard, for serving

Contents per piece

Calories	32
Total fat	0.8 g
saturated fat	0.3 g
monounsaturated fat	0.4 g
polyunsaturated fat	0.1 g
Protein	2.6 g
Carbohydrates	3.5 g
Cholesterol	20 mg
Fiber	0.1 g
Calories from fat	23%

1 Preheat oven to 350 F.

2 Cut the sausages into 1" pieces. Spray a mini muffin pan (use two if you have them) with non-stick spray and put a piece of sausage into each cup. Stand the sausage upright if you can. Bake for about 10 minutes, until they're beginning to brown. Turn the oven up to 450 F.

3 In a medium bowl, whisk together the flour, milk, egg, salt and pepper until relatively smooth.

4 Remove the sausages from the oven and quickly pour a scant tablespoon of batter around each sausage. Return the pan to the oven for 15 - 20 minutes, until puffed and golden. Serve them warm, with a dish of grainy mustard for people to dab on top if they like.

Makes about 16 mini Toad-in-the-Holes.

Mini Yorkshire Puddings with Roast Beef & Horseradish Cream

Bake the batter in the muffin cups without the sausage. Top each mini Yorkshire pudding with a little pile of thinly sliced deli roast beef. Stir 1 - 2 Tbsp prepared horseradish or grainy mustard into 1 cup low fat sour cream and top each pudding with a small dollop of it.

Goong Waan (Sweet & Spicy Shrimp)

This is a variation of a recipe from Sheila Lukins' wonderful *All Around the World* cookbook. She credits it to a cooking class in Bangkok. Make sure you use peeled shrimp with the tails left on to use as a handle – if you use shrimp in their shells, the shells fuse to the meat!

1 lb large tail-on shrimp

1/2 cup packed brown sugar

1/4 cup water

3 Tbsp fish sauce

2 cloves garlic, crushed

1/4 tsp ground white pepper

2 Tbsp chopped fresh cilantro (optional)

Contents per serving

Calories	226
Total fat	1.5 g
saturated fat	0.4 g
monounsaturated fat	0.3 g
polyunsaturated fat	0.8 g
Protein	23.1 g
Carbohydrates	28.3 g
Cholesterol	172.4 mg
Fiber	0.0 g
Calories from fat	8%

1. In a medium saucepan, combine water, brown sugar and fish sauce. Cook over medium heat for a few minutes until the sugar dissolves.

2. Add the garlic and pepper and bring to a boil. Reduce heat and simmer until the sauce reduces and thickens, about 8 - 10 minutes.

3. Add the shrimp and cook, stirring and flipping them constantly, just until they turn pink. This should only take a minute or two. Transfer to a bowl, sprinkle with cilantro and set aside to cool.

4. Refrigerate shrimp until chilled, and transfer to a serving bowl with a slotted spoon. Serve with lots of napkins and an extra bowl for the tails.

Serves 4.

Curried Peanut Shrimp

Throw the shrimp and marinade into a baggie in the morning and you'll have dinner almost ready when you come home from work. Sometimes I simmer the whole lot, sauce and all, in a large sauté pan and serve it over rice to catch the sauce.

1/4 cup orange marmalade

1/4 cup orange juice

2 Tbsp light peanut butter

1 tsp curry paste

1 tsp sesame or canola oil

1 clove garlic, crushed

1/2 tsp chili sauce or sambal oelek

1/4 tsp salt

pinch red pepper flakes

1/2 lb large shrimp, peeled and deveined, with the tails left on

1 Combine everything but the shrimp in a bowl or jar and whisk or shake until smooth. Pour over the shrimp in a container or zip-lock bag and marinate in the fridge for an hour or overnight.

2 When ready to cook, spray a large non-stick sauté pan with non-stick spray and set over medium heat. Add the shrimp and cook for a few minutes on each side, just until they turn pink. (If you want, you could thread the shrimp onto bamboo skewers that have been soaked in water. Place on a grill rack or broiler pan that has been sprayed with non-stick spray and cook for about 3 minutes on each side.) Simmer the reserved marinade in a small saucepan for a few minutes and serve alongside the shrimp for dipping.

Serves 4.

Contents per serving

Calories	159
Total fat	4.4 g
saturated fat	0.8 g
monounsaturated fat	1.8 g
polyunsaturated fat	1.8 g
Protein	13.2 g
Carbohydrates	16.5 g
Cholesterol	86.2 mg
Fiber	0.4 g
Calories from fat	27%

Basic Pizza Crust

Pizza dough is a wonderfully versatile thing. I know you can buy pre-baked crusts at the grocery store for a few dollars, but pizza crust made from scratch is far better, costs practically nothing, and I find the process of mixing and kneading the dough by hand therapeutic and greatly satisfying. Once the dough has risen it can be twisted into bread sticks or pretzels, patted into focaccia, or topped with whatever you like and baked into a pizza or flatbread. To boost fiber, replace half the flour with whole wheat flour. For crunchier dough, substitute 1/2 cup cornmeal for 1/2 cup of the flour.

1 cup lukewarm water

1 package or 2¼ tsp active dry yeast

1 tsp sugar or honey

2½ - 3 cups flour
(I usually use about 23/4 cups)

1 tsp salt

1 tsp - 1 Tbsp olive oil

Contents per slice (6 slices per pizza)

Calories	111
Total fat	0.6 g
saturated fat	0.1 g
monounsaturated fat	0.3 g
polyunsaturated fat	0.2 g
Protein	3.2 g
Carbohydrates	22.5 g
Cholesterol	0.0 mg
Fiber	1.1 g
Calories from fat	6%

1. In a large bowl, stir together the water, yeast and sugar; set aside for 5 minutes, until it's foamy. (If it doesn't get foamy, either your water was too hot and killed the yeast or it was inactive to begin with – toss it and try again or buy fresh yeast!)

2. Add 2½ cups flour, salt and oil and stir until the dough comes together. On a lightly floured surface, knead the dough for about 8 minutes, until it's smooth and elastic, adding a little more flour if the dough is too sticky.

3. Place the dough in an oiled bowl and turn to coat all over. Cover with a tea towel or plastic wrap and set aside in a warm place for about 1 hour, until doubled in bulk. If you want, you can let it rise more slowly in the refrigerator for up to 8 hours.

4. Punch the dough down, cover again, and let it rest for 5 minutes. Divide in half and shape each half into a circle (or make individual mini-pizzas). Place on a cookie sheet that has been sprinkled with cornmeal.

Clockwise from bottom left:
Berry Whole Wheat White Chocolate Drop Scones
One Bite Brownies
Sticky Biscuits
Ginger Molasses Crinkles

Clockwise from bottom left:
Cranberry, Orange and White Chocolate Chunk Cookies
Chocolate Swirl Banana Bread
Peppermint Patties

Clockwise from bottom left:
Stone Fruit Tarts
Breakfast Bean Cookies
Bagels with Cranberry Orange Goat Cheese Schmear
Peanut Butter Power Bars

Clockwise from bottom right:
Browned Butter, Pistachio and Olive Biscotti
Caramelized Onion Dip
Pretzel Nuggets
Olive & Garlic Breadsticks
Flaxseed Wafers

BBQ Chicken Pizza

Pizza can be made with anything you have on hand – if you don't have tomato sauce, use BBQ sauce. If you don't have mozzarella, use up any bits of cheese you have in the back of the fridge. If you have kids around, BBQ chicken pizza will be an instant hit.

5 Let the crust rise another half-hour while you prepare the toppings. Spread the pizza dough with tomato sauce, sprinkle with desired toppings and bake at 450 F for 15 - 20 minutes, until bubbly and golden.

Makes enough dough for 2 - 9" pizzas.

Flavored Pizza Dough

Add a generous pinch of chopped fresh or dried basil, rosemary or oregano, a clove of minced garlic, a few finely chopped olives or sun-dried tomatoes (if they come packed in oil, use it in place of the olive oil) or 1/2 tsp freshly ground black pepper along with the flour. Flavored pizza dough makes great breadsticks – roll the risen dough into sticks as thin or fat as you like, sprinkle with coarse salt or grated Parmesan cheese, and bake until golden.

1 batch pizza dough (see page 92)

3/4 cup barbecue sauce

1 cup roasted chicken, skinned and chopped or shredded

1 cup shredded part-skim mozzarella cheese, sharp white cheddar, Gouda, or a combination

1 green onion, chopped

2 Tbsp chopped fresh cilantro (optional)

1 Preheat oven to 350 F.

2 In a small bowl, toss the chicken with 1/4 cup barbecue sauce.

3 Spread the unbaked pizza crusts with remaining barbecue sauce. Top with the chicken mixture, cheese and green onion. Bake for 15 - 20 minutes or until the cheese melts and crust is golden. Sprinkle with cilantro.

Makes 2 - 9" pizzas (6 slices each).

Contents per slice

Calories	180
Total fat	2.6 g
saturated fat	1.2 g
monounsaturated fat	0.9 g
polyunsaturated fat	0.5 g
Protein	12.3 g
Carbohydrates	25 g
Cholesterol	21 mg
Fiber	2.1 g
Calories from fat	15%

Caramelized Onion, Feta & Olive Pizza

Homemade pizza sounds like a lot of work, but it really isn't a big deal. Once you've made your own, you'll never bother with frozen pizza or takeout again! Pizza dough doubles easily and freezes well, so if you only want one pizza, freeze half the dough for later. If you need to feed a crowd, double the recipe. If you're in a rush, you can get away with buying frozen bread dough or prebaked pizza crusts just this once.

1 batch pizza dough (see page 92)

1 Tbsp olive or canola oil

6 cups thinly sliced onions

freshly ground black pepper to taste

1 garlic clove, crushed

1 cup (about 4 oz) crumbled feta or goat cheese

1/4 cup coarsely chopped pitted Kalamata olives

1 Preheat oven to 350 F.

2 In a large non-stick pan, sauté the onions in oil over medium-low heat for about 20 minutes, until caramelized. Stir in the garlic and pepper for the last minute of cooking.

3 Spread the caramelized onions on the unbaked pizza crusts and sprinkle with feta and olives. Bake for 15 - 20 minutes, until golden and the cheese melts.

Makes 2 - 9" pizzas.

Contents per slice

Calories	176
Total fat	4.1 g
saturated fat	1.8 g
monounsaturated fat	1.8 g
polyunsaturated fat	0.5 g
Protein	5.4 g
Carbohydrates	28.8 g
Cholesterol	8.7 mg
Fiber	2.3 g
Calories from fat	22%

Potato Skins

This may seem like an obvious recipe, but cheesy potato skins are a quintessential finger food and people don't often make them at home. The spice mixture adds a lot of flavor, and Canadian bacon is much leaner than the breakfast variety. I always use intensely flavored cheeses, like old cheddar, instead of the low-fat kind, which tends to be rubbery with very little flavor.

4 medium baking potatoes
(russets work well and have sturdy skins)

1 - 2 Tbsp olive or canola oil

1/4 tsp each salt & pepper

1/2 tsp each chili powder
and curry powder (optional)

1/4 cup chopped Canadian bacon
or turkey pepperoni

2 green onions, chopped

3/4 cup shredded old cheddar cheese

salsa and low fat sour cream

Contents per serving

Calories	115
Total fat	6.8 g
saturated fat	2.8 g
monounsaturated fat	3.6 g
polyunsaturated fat	0.4 g
Protein	5.1 g
Carbohydrates	7.9 g
Cholesterol	16.0 mg
Fiber	1.1 g
Calories from fat	55%

1. Preheat oven to 400 F.

2. Bake the potatoes whole for about an hour, until tender. Set aside until cool enough to handle.

3. Cut each potato in quarters lengthwise and scoop out the pulp, leaving a 1/4" thick shell. (Keep the potato for something else – I always fry it up in a little oil the next morning with what's left of the spice mixture). Place potato skins on a baking sheet and brush with oil. Combine the salt, pepper, chili and curry powder and sprinkle over top. Bake for another 10 minutes, until crispy.

4. Sprinkle with bacon, green onions and cheese, and bake for another 5 minutes, until the cheese melts. Serve with salsa and low-fat sour cream.

Serves 4.

Green Eggs with Ham

OK, so I developed this recipe just so I could use the name. But it turned out to be one of my favorites! Spinach, eggs, ham and cheese are a great combo. These are really intensely flavored little bites.

6 large eggs

1 tsp canola oil

2 slices deli ham, chopped or julienned

a handful of fresh spinach or chard, chopped

1 Tbsp light mayonnaise

2 Tbsp grated Parmesan cheese

salt and pepper to taste

Contents per piece

Calories	55
Total fat	3.2 g
saturated fat	1.1 g
monounsaturated fat	1.5 g
polyunsaturated fat	0.6 g
Protein	4.5 g
Carbohydrates	0.8 g
Cholesterol	111.0 mg
Fiber	0.1 g
Calories from fat	61%

1. Place the eggs in a medium saucepan. Cover with water and bring to a boil. Cover, remove from heat and let stand 15 minutes. Drain and rinse with cold water until cool. Peel and slice in half lengthwise. Remove yolks and set 3 aside for another use.

2. Meanwhile, heat the oil in a saucepan set over medium heat and sauté the ham for a minute. Add the spinach and cook for another minute, until wilted.

3. In a medium bowl mash 3 yolks with the mayonnaise, Parmesan cheese, salt and pepper until smooth. Add the spinach mixture and stir until well blended.

4. Stuff egg white halves with filling and serve immediately.

Makes 12.

Smoked Salmon Deviled Eggs

It seems everyone gets excited over deviled eggs – at a party they're always the first to go. Eggs aren't as bad for you as you might think – they are lower in cholesterol than was once thought, and of the 5 grams of fat a large yolk contains, only 1 gram is saturated. (Research has shown that saturated fat has a worse effect on blood cholesterol levels than dietary cholesterol does.) They are also a great source of protein. These recipes eliminate half the yolks and replace them with more flavorful ingredients.

small russet potato, peeled and diced

5 large eggs

1/2 cup smoked or BBQ salmon tip, crumbled

Tbsp light mayonnaise

tsp fresh lemon juice

tsp grainy mustard

green onion, finely chopped

salt and pepper to taste

Contents per piece

Calories	65
Total fat	2.8 g
saturated fat	0.9 g
monounsaturated fat	1.3 g
polyunsaturated fat	0.6 g
Protein	5.8 g
Carbohydrates	2.9 g
Cholesterol	114.0 mg
Fiber	0.3 g
Calories from fat	47%

1 Cook potato in a pot of boiling salted water until very tender. Drain and cool.

2 Meanwhile, place eggs in a medium saucepan. Cover with water and bring to a boil. Cover, remove from heat and let stand 15 minutes. Drain and rinse with cold water until cool. Peel and slice in half lengthwise. Remove yolks and set 3 aside for another use, or feed them to your dog.

3 In a medium bowl combine the remaining yolks, potato, salmon, mayonnaise, lemon juice and mustard; mash with fork until well blended. Stir in the green onion, salt and pepper.

4 Stuff egg white halves with filling and chill until ready to serve.

Makes 12.

Balsamic Mushroom Crostini

My friend Sue and I used to sauté loads of mushrooms in butter late and night and eat big bowls of them. This appetizer is a little more sophisticated and a lot lower in fat, but almost as easy to put together. If you have friends coming over it looks like you went to a lot of fuss. It's a perfect example of maximum reward for minimum effort.

18 slices baguette, sliced diagonally about $1/2$" thick

1 large clove garlic, cut in half lengthwise

1 Tbsp canola oil

6 cups sliced fresh mushrooms – button, Portobello, shitake or a combination

salt and pepper to taste

$1/4$ cup dried cranberries

2 Tbsp balsamic vinegar

1 Tbsp fresh rosemary, chopped

$1/2$ cup shredded Asiago, aged gouda or old white cheddar cheese

Contents per crostini

Calories	84
Total fat	1.8 g
saturated fat	0.5 g
monounsaturated fat	0.9 g
polyunsaturated fat	0.4 g
Protein	2.9 g
Carbohydrates	13.7 g
Cholesterol	1.6 mg
Fiber	1.0 g
Calories from fat	22%

1. Preheat oven to 400 F.

2. Place baguette slices on a cookie sheet and toast in the oven for about 10 minutes, until barely golden. If you like, brush each toast with olive oil before baking. Rub each slice with the cut side of the clove of garlic.

3. Heat oil in a large non-stick skillet set over medium-high heat. Cook the mushrooms, stirring occasionally, until the moisture has evaporated. Season with salt and pepper and continue to cook until the mushrooms are golden. Add the cranberries, balsamic vinegar and rosemary and cook for another minute, until the liquid has evaporated.

4. Spoon the hot mixture onto toasts and sprinkle with cheese. Return to the oven for 5 minutes, until the cheese melts.

Makes about 18 crostini.

Balsamic Mushroom Dip

Stir 4 oz light cream cheese or goat cheese and $1/2$ cup light sour cream into the mushroom mixture while it's still warm, and stir over low heat until the cheese melts. Serve warm with crackers or crostini for dipping.

Roasted Pearl Onion Crostini

These are like little French onion soup bites you can eat with your hands. If you're a garlic fan, peel some cloves and roast them along with the onions. This recipe can easily be halved or doubled.

2 lbs pearl onions

2 Tbsp olive oil

salt and freshly ground pepper

1 baguette, sliced on an angle 1/4" thick

1/2 cup grated Parmesan cheese

1 Tbsp balsamic vinegar

Contents per crostini

Calories	114
Total fat	2.4 g
saturated fat	0.7 g
monounsaturated fat	1.4 g
polyunsaturated fat	0.3 g
Protein	3.9 g
Carbohydrates	18.5 g
Cholesterol	1.6 mg
Fiber	1.4 g
Calories from fat	21%

1 Preheat oven to 450 F.

2 Bring a medium pot of water to a boil. Add the onions and blanch for about 30 seconds; drain and run under cold water. Peel them and trim off the roots.

3 On a large, rimmed baking sheet, toss the onions with 1 Tbsp of the olive oil and season with salt and pepper. Roast the onions for about 30 minutes, stirring once or twice, until they are caramelized and softened.

4 Arrange the baguette slices on a baking sheet and brush with the remaining olive oil. Sprinkle with Parmesan cheese and bake for about 5 minutes, until the cheese is melted and the bread is crisp.

5 Sprinkle the onions with vinegar, salt and pepper. Pile the onions on the cheese toasts and serve warm or at room temperature.

Makes about 2 dozen crostini.

Roasted Pearl Onion Crostini with Cambozola
Omit the Parmesan cheese. Pile the roasted onions on the crostini and top with a thin slice of Cambozola. Return to the oven for a few minutes, just until the cheese melts.

Bruschetta

The term bruschetta (pronounced either "brusketta" or "brushetta") comes from the Italian bruscare, meaning "to roast over coals", and traditionally refers to toasted bread rubbed with garlic and drizzled with olive oil. But in Canada when someone says "bruschetta", they are more often referring to a salsa-like mixture of tomatoes, garlic and oil, served on a slice of toasted baguette.

4 ripe tomatoes, diced (make sure they're good quality – flavor is important here!)

1 - 2 cloves garlic, crushed

1 - 4 Tbsp good quality olive oil

1 Tbsp balsamic vinegar

1/4 cup finely chopped fresh basil

salt & freshly ground pepper to taste

**18 crostini (see page 43)
or toasted baguette slices**

1 Mix everything but the crostini together in a large bowl. Spoon onto crostini or serve in a bowl along with the crostini so that people can serve themselves.

Makes about 18 pieces.

Smashed Cherry Tomato and Olive Bruschetta

Use a pint of cherry tomatoes and 1/4 cup pitted Kalamata olives instead of the 4 ripe tomatoes, and smash them with a potato masher. Add everything else.

Contents per piece

Calories	28
Total fat	1.1 g
saturated fat	0.2 g
monounsaturated fat	0.8 g
polyunsaturated fat	0.1 g
Protein	0.7 g
Carbohydrates	4.0 g
Cholesterol	0 mg
Fiber	0.5 g
Calories from fat	36%

White Bean, Tomato & Olive Bruschetta with Goat Cheese

Bring a container of this bruschetta and a chunk of baguette to work for lunch, or to the park or beach for a picnic. To get the pits out of olives, smash them on a board with the flat side of your knife.

1 - 19 oz (540 mL) can white kidney beans, rinsed and drained

3 ripe plum tomatoes, seeded and chopped

1/4 - 1/2 cup Kalamata olives, pitted and chopped

1/4 cup chopped fresh basil

2 Tbsp olive oil

1 Tbsp balsamic vinegar

2 cloves garlic, crushed

salt and pepper to taste

24 crostini (page 43) or toasted baguette slices

4 oz soft fresh goat cheese, grated Pecorino Romano or Parmesan cheese (optional)

1 In a medium bowl, lightly crush the beans with a fork, keeping them chunky. Stir in the tomatoes, olives, basil, olive oil, balsamic vinegar, garlic, salt and pepper. Stir until well blended.

2 If you are using goat cheese, spread it on the toasts and spoon the bean mixture on top. If you are using Romano cheese, spoon the bean mixture onto the toasts and sprinkle the grated cheese on top. Pop them into the oven until the cheese melts if you like.

Makes about 2 dozen pieces.

Contents per piece

Calories	58
Total fat	1.6 g
saturated fat	0.2 g
monounsaturated fat	1.2 g
polyunsaturated fat	0.2 g
Protein	2.5 g
Carbohydrates	8.4 g
Cholesterol	0 mg
Fiber	1.8 g
Calories from fat	27%

Tomato, Avocado & Shrimp Bruschetta

Chicken, Black Bean & Mushroom Quesadilla

If you can make a grilled cheese sandwich, you can make a quesadilla! They are a little trickier to flip – if you have trouble, slide the quesadilla onto a plate, and then invert it back into the pan.

1 lb cooked, peeled shrimp

2 - 3 ripe tomatoes, seeded and chopped

1 ripe avocado, peeled and chopped

1 Tbsp lemon juice

3 Tbsp chopped fresh basil

2 cloves garlic, minced

1 Tbsp olive oil

salt and pepper to taste

18 crostini (page 43) or toasted baguette slices

1 Coarsely chop the shrimp if they are large. Place in a large bowl with tomatoes, avocado, lemon juice, basil, garlic and olive oil. Add pepper and salt and toss gently until well combined.

2 Spoon onto top of crostini or baguette.

Makes about 18 pieces.

Contents per piece

Calories	70
Total fat	2.9 g
saturated fat	0.5 g
monounsaturated fat	1.9 g
polyunsaturated fat	0.5 g
Protein	5.9 g
Carbohydrates	4.5 g
Cholesterol	38.3 mg
Fiber	0.6 g
Calories from fat	42%

4 - 10" flour tortillas

1 Tbsp canola oil or butter

1 small onion, finely chopped

3 cups sliced mushrooms

3 cloves garlic, crushed

1 cup chopped cooked chicken

1/2 - 19 oz (540 mL) can black beans, rinsed and drained

1/2 tsp ground cumin

1/2 tsp salt

1 1/2 cups grated old cheddar cheese

Contents per serving

Calories	355
Total fat	10.8 g
saturated fat	5.1 g
monounsaturated fat	3.8 g
polyunsaturated fat	1.9 g
Protein	24.2 g
Carbohydrates	38.4 g
Cholesterol	45.8 mg
Fiber	6.3 g
Calories from fat	30%

Quesadilla Variations

People tend to get more creative with their fillings when making quesadillas than they do with grilled cheese sandwiches. Basically you can put anything inside – just make sure there is enough cheese to keep it together.

1 Heat the oil in a large skillet set over medium heat and sauté the onions for a few minutes, until soft. Add the mushrooms and garlic and cook until the mushrooms are golden and the moisture has evaporated. Add the chicken, beans, cumin and salt and stir until well blended. Remove from heat.

2 Place a flour tortilla in a large dry skillet set over medium heat and spread with 1/4 cup of cheese, half the chicken mixture and another 1/4 cup cheese. Top with a second tortilla. Cook, shaking the pan gently and pressing the top to help it seal, until the bottom is golden and the cheese is melting. Flip the quesadilla. Cook for another few minutes, until golden on the other side and the cheese is melted. Slide onto a plate and repeat with the remaining tortillas, chicken and cheese.

3 Cut into wedges and serve with salsa and light sour cream.

Serves 4.

- BBQ duck (buy it in Chinatown), hoisin sauce, grated mozzarella and fresh cilantro
- Roasted vegetables with any kind of cheese
- Caramelized onions, Kalamata olives and feta cheese
- Cheddar cheese, purple onion & tomato
- Black beans, chopped mango & feta cheese
- Chopped cooked chicken, grated old cheddar or mozzarella cheese, thinly sliced purple onion, BBQ sauce and fresh cilantro

California Rolls (Sushi with Avocado and Crab)

I'm not very daring when it comes to sushi – I usually stick to California rolls while my friends tuck in to sashimi and smoked eel. I discovered after a friend took a sushi making class that California rolls aren't very difficult to make. They are also very delicious and very low in calories. You'll need a Bamboo sushi mat, which you'll find at most kitchen stores, usually for a dollar or two.

1 cup long grain rice

¼ cup rice vinegar

1 Tbsp sugar

1 tsp salt

1 avocado, peeled, pitted and cut into long, thin slices

OR 1 small English cucumber, peeled, seeded and cut into long, thin slices

2 Tbsp lemon juice

6 sheets nori (seaweed)

½ lb Alaskan king crab meat or imitation crab (pollock)

¼ cup light mayonnaise (optional)

For Dipping

¼ cup soy sauce

2 Tbsp rice wine

Contents per piece

Calories	37
Total fat	1.0 g
saturated fat	0.2 g
monounsaturated fat	0.6 g
polyunsaturated fat	0.2 g
Protein	1.8 g
Carbohydrates	5.2 g
Cholesterol	3.3 mg
Fiber	0.2 g
Calories from fat	24%

1. Wash the rice in several changes of cold water until the water runs clear. Drain it well and combine it with 1½ cups water in a heavy saucepan. Let it stand for 30 minutes, then bring it to a boil, cover and simmer over low heat for 10 minutes. Turn the heat up to high for another minute and then remove from heat. Let the rice stand, covered, for 15 more minutes and then transfer it to a large bowl.

2. Combine the rice vinegar, sugar and salt in a small saucepan or microwave safe-bowl and cook for a few minutes, until the sugar is dissolved. Cool and add to the warm rice, stirring gently. Let the rice cool completely before you use it.

3. Toss the avocado with lemon juice to keep it from discoloring, and toss the crabmeat with mayonnaise if you're using it.

4. Lay a bamboo sushi mat on the counter with the slats running horizontally. Put a piece of the nori on it with the nori's long side facing you. With dampened hands, spread ½ cup of the rice over it, leaving a 1" border across the top edge.

5 Arrange 3 avocado slices, overlapping them a bit, in a horizontal line across the middle of the rice and top with about 1/6th of the crab. Grab the edge of the mat closest to you and roll the nori away from you as tightly as you can, pressing the roll as you go so it keeps its shape. Dip your finger in some water and moisten the far edge of the nori, and press, to seal. Transfer to a cutting board and make rolls with the remaining ingredients.

6 With a sharp, serrated knife dipped in hot water, cut the rolls into 1" slices, trimming off the ends. Stir together the soy sauce and rice wine and serve alongside the rolls with a little wasabi and pickled ginger.

Makes 36 pieces.

Food on a Stick

Who doesn't love food served on a stick? Corn dogs, popsicles, fudgesicles and caramel apples all evoke fond childhood memories. Threading your food onto a stick is a great way to enforce portion control too – you can actually count how many skewers you've gone through!

Poking a skewer through any kind of food immediately fancies it up, which makes it perfect for parties. And with no utensils, no one wonders how to serve themselves. Most of these recipes can be made in advance and refrigerated or frozen until you're ready to grill or broil them – a bonus if you are expecting company and a lifesaver if you don't have extra time yourself. (Who does?) But don't wait for a party – food on a stick is great any day. Satays became one of my staple meals while I was writing this book because I always had a stash in the freezer.

Chicken Satay with Peanut Sauce

Moist and flavorful chicken satays are perfect for a party or make a great dinner. Serve them with the peanut sauce on the next page. I couldn't decide which of my favorite marinades to include, so here are both!

1¹/2 lbs skinless, boneless chicken breasts or beef fillet, cut into strips

Marinade #1

2 Tbsp soy sauce

2 Tbsp lemon juice

1 Tbsp honey

1 tsp sesame oil

2 cloves garlic, crushed

1 tsp grated fresh ginger

1 tsp curry paste (optional)

Marinade #2

¹/2 cup plain yogurt

1 small onion, grated (optional)

3 cloves garlic, crushed

1 Tbsp grated fresh ginger

1 Tbsp soy sauce

1 Tbsp brown sugar or honey

1 Tbsp curry powder

¹/2 tsp cumin

1 Cut chicken lengthwise into strips and place in a bowl or zip-lock bag. Combine all the marinade ingredients and pour over the chicken; toss well to coat and refrigerate for an hour or overnight.

2 Thread the chicken onto bamboo skewers that have been soaked in water for at least 10 minutes. Grill or broil for a few minutes on each side, until just cooked through. Serve warm, at room temperature, or cold with Peanut Sauce (see page 109) for dipping

Makes about 20 satays.

Contents per satay with marinade	#1	#2
Calories	49	46
Total fat	1.1 g	0.5 g
saturated fat	0.3 g	0.2 g
monounsaturated fat	0.4 g	0.2 g
polyunsaturated fat	0.4 g	0.1 g
Protein	7.7 g	7.8 g
Carbohydrates	1.4 g	1.5 g
Cholesterol	19.7 mg	20 mg
Fiber	0.0 g	0.1 g
Calories from fat	24%	14%

Peanut Sauce

This popular sauce is great with Chicken or Pork Satay (see page 110), Teriyaki Beef Sticks (see page 115) and Vietnamese Rice Paper Rolls (see page 127). I also love to dip green grapes in peanut sauce.

2 - 4 Tbsp chicken or veggie broth or water

3 Tbsp light peanut butter

3 Tbsp soy sauce

2 Tbsp brown sugar or honey

2 Tbsp rice vinegar or lime juice

1 - 2 cloves garlic, crushed

1 - 2 tsp grated fresh ginger

1 tsp sesame oil (optional)

¼ - ½ tsp curry paste (optional)

1 Combine all the ingredients in a blender or jar and whiz or shake until smooth. Refrigerate until you're ready to serve it.

Makes about 1 cup.

Contents per Tbsp

Calories	26
Total fat	1.1 g
saturated fat	0.2 g
monounsaturated fat	0.5 g
polyunsaturated fat	0.4 g
Protein	0.7 g
Carbohydrates	3.9 g
Cholesterol	0.0 mg
Fiber	0.0 g
Calories from fat	35%

Pork Satay

These are perfect if you want something to make in advance – the longer they marinate the more flavorful they become. You could also use beef sirloin, sliced into strips. I always bring a baggie of marinating strips and some bamboo skewers to barbecues and grill them there. They're also great to bring camping or to the cabin.

2 pork tenderloins, trimmed of fat (about 1¹/2 lbs)

¹/4 cup orange juice

¹/4 cup soy sauce

2 Tbsp lime or lemon juice

1 Tbsp packed brown sugar

3 cloves garlic, crushed

1 Tbsp grated fresh ginger

1 tsp curry powder
and/or ¹/2 tsp ground cumin

2 green onions, chopped

1 Combine everything but the pork in a medium bowl. Cut the pork into strips and add to the marinade, stirring well to coat. Cover and refrigerate for 2 hours or overnight.

2 Soak bamboo skewers in water while the pork is marinating. Thread strips of pork onto the skewers and grill or broil for about 3 minutes per side, just until cooked through. Serve hot, warm or cold with Peanut Sauce (see page 109) for dipping.

Makes about 18 satays.

Contents per satay

Calories	56
Total fat	0.8 g
saturated fat	0.3 g
monounsaturated fat	0.4 g
polyunsaturated fat	0.1 g
Protein	9.3 g
Carbohydrates	1.2 g
Cholesterol	22.3 mg
Fiber	0.2 g
Calories from fat	16%

Tandoori Chicken Satay

For an even faster marinade, stir 1/2 cup of prepared tandoori paste into the plain yogurt.

1 lb skinless, boneless chicken breasts, cut into strips

1/4 cup plain yogurt

1 small onion, grated or finely chopped

1 Tbsp olive oil

1 Tbsp grated fresh ginger

2 cloves garlic, crushed

1/4 tsp coriander

1/4 tsp cumin

1/4 tsp turmeric

1/4 tsp cayenne pepper

1/4 tsp each salt and pepper

1 Put everything in a bowl and mix well. Refrigerate for at least 2 hours or overnight, stirring or shaking occasionally. Soak 12 bamboo skewers in water for at least 10 minutes to prevent them from burning.

2 Remove the chicken from the bag and discard the marinade. Thread chicken strips onto the skewers. Grill or broil on a pan coated with non-stick spray for a few minutes on each side, just until done.

Makes about 12 satays.

Contents per satay

Calories	51
Total fat	1.0 g
saturated fat	0.3 g
monounsaturated fat	0.5 g
polyunsaturated fat	0.2 g
Protein	8.8 g
Carbohydrates	0.8 g
Cholesterol	22.2 mg
Fiber	0.1 g
Calories from fat	20%

Jerk Chicken Skewers

Although the ingredient list is long, these are a snap to put together. If you want to prep them far in advance, freeze the baggie full of chicken and marinade for up to three months; thaw before threading onto skewers and grilling.

1 lb skinless, boneless chicken breast or pork tenderloin

4 green onions, chopped

2 cloves garlic, crushed

1 jalapeño or small hot red pepper, seeded and chopped

2 Tbsp orange or lime juice

2 Tbsp soy sauce

1 Tbsp canola oil

1/2 tsp allspice

1/2 tsp thyme

1/2 tsp curry powder

1/4 tsp cinnamon

1/4 tsp ground ginger

1/4 tsp nutmeg

1/4 tsp salt

1/4 tsp pepper

1 Combine everything but the chicken in the bowl of a food processor or blender and whiz until well blended and relatively smooth. Cut the chicken into strips and put them in a bowl or zip-lock bag; pour the marinade over and stir to coat well. Put it in the fridge for at least 1 hour or leave it overnight.

2 Thread the chicken onto 12 wooden skewers that have been soaked in water for at least 10 minutes to prevent them from burning. Grill or broil for about 5 minutes per side, until cooked through. Serve warm.

Makes about a dozen skewers.

Contents per skewer

Calories	62
Total fat	1.6 g
saturated fat	0.3 g
monounsaturated fat	0.8 g
polyunsaturated fat	0.5 g
Protein	8.9 g
Carbohydrates	2.3 g
Cholesterol	21.9 mg
Fiber	0.5 g
Calories from fat	28%

BBQ Buffalo Chicken Strips with Blue Cheese Dip

I like to use a mild, tomato-based BBQ sauce when I make these – it allows the flavor of the hot sauce to come through. If you want to make them in advance, you can freeze the dipped chicken strips on a baking sheet, then transfer to a plastic bag. When you're ready to bake them, place the frozen strips on a cookie sheet and bake as directed – there's no need to thaw them first.

1 lb skinless, boneless chicken breasts, cut into strips

1/4 cup flour

salt and pepper to taste

1/2 cup barbecue sauce

2 - 4 Tbsp hot pepper sauce
(such as Frank's Red Hot sauce)

Blue Cheese Dip

1/2 cup low fat sour cream or plain yogurt

2 Tbsp light mayonnaise

2 oz blue cheese, crumbled

1 green onion, finely chopped

1 Preheat oven to 400 F.

2 Season flour with salt and pepper in a shallow dish. Stir together the barbecue sauce and hot sauce in another dish.

3 Dredge chicken strips in the flour to coat, then dip into the barbecue sauce mixture and turn to coat all over. Place on a baking sheet that has been sprayed with non-stick spray.

4 Bake for 20 minutes, or until cooked through. To make the blue cheese dip, stir together all the dip ingredients. Bottled low-fat ranch or creamy cucumber dressing is good too.

Makes about a dozen strips.

Contents per strip

Calories	60
Total fat	0.6 g
saturated fat	0.2 g
monounsaturated fat	0.2 g
polyunsaturated fat	0.2 g
Protein	8.9 g
Carbohydrates	3.4 g
Cholesterol	21.9 mg
Fiber	0.7 g
Calories from fat	14%

Greek Lamb Kebabs

Serve these with yogurt mint sauce for dipping, or stuff into a fresh pita with crumbled feta, chopped tomato, cucumber, purple onion and lots of tzatziki (see page 70).

1 lb ground lamb or lean ground beef

1 small onion, peeled and grated

1/2 cup soft bread crumbs (about 1 slice of bread), bulgur or couscous

4 cloves garlic, crushed

1 large egg

2 Tbsp chopped pine nuts

2 Tbsp chopped raisins (optional)

1 Tbsp grated fresh ginger

1 tsp cumin

1/2 tsp salt

1/4 tsp ground cinnamon

small handful chopped fresh flat-leaf parsley, cilantro or mint (optional)

1 Preheat oven to 400 F.

2 Soak some bamboo skewers in water for at least 10 minutes.

3 Combine all the ingredients in a large bowl. Shape handfuls of the meat mixture into flattened sausages about 4" long around the ends of the skewers. Grill over medium-high heat, turning often and brushing with a bit of olive oil, until cooked through.

4 Serve warm or cold with yogurt mint sauce (see below) or tzatziki (see page 70) for dipping.

Makes 6 kebabs.

Yogurt Mint Sauce
Stir 2 Tbsp chopped fresh mint, a crushed clove of garlic and 1 Tbsp each of olive oil and lemon juice into 1 cup good quality plain yogurt. Season with salt and pepper.

Greek Meatballs
Shape mixture into balls and place 1/2" apart on a baking pan or rimmed cookie sheet. Bake for 15 - 20 minutes, until cooked through. (You could also cook them in a non-stick skillet until they're done.) Makes about 20 meatballs. Serve warm or cold with yogurt mint sauce or tzatziki (see page 70) for dipping.

Contents per kebab

Calories	224
Total fat	7.2 g
saturated fat	2.9 g
monounsaturated fat	3.3 g
polyunsaturated fat	1.0 g
Protein	26.6 g
Carbohydrates	8.9 g
Cholesterol	128.7 mg
Fiber	0.4 g
Calories from fat	34%

Teriyaki Beef Sticks

You can often find packages of 'stir fry' beef at the grocery store that's already been cut into strips. Sometimes when I get it home from the store I pop the beef into a zip-lock bag, pour the marinade over it and stick it in the freezer. That way I always have something easy on hand for myself or for company.

1 lb lean boneless top round or skirt steak, cut into strips

1/4 cup soy sauce

1/4 cup honey or brown sugar

2 cloves garlic, crushed

2 Tbsp grated fresh ginger

1 Tbsp lime or lemon juice

Contents per stick

Calories	55
Total fat	1.2 g
saturated fat	0.5 g
monounsaturated fat	0.6 g
polyunsaturated fat	0.1 g
Protein	5.3 g
Carbohydrates	5.1 g
Cholesterol	15.1 mg
Fiber	0.0 g
Calories from fat	24%

1. Combine soy sauce, honey, garlic, ginger and lime juice and pour over the beef; stir to coat well and refrigerate for a few hours or overnight.

2. Thread beef onto bamboo skewers that have been soaked in water for at least 20 minutes. Grill or pan-fry for a few minutes on each side, brushing with remaining marinade, until just cooked through.

3. Serve plain or with peanut sauce (see page 109) for dipping.

Makes about 18 skewers.

Honey, Ginger & Sesame Salmon Sticks

To me, these are like candy on a stick. I'd eat the whole lot if no one was around to fight me for them. Salmon is a fatty fish, rich in omega-3 fatty acids, which fight heart disease by lowering triglyceride levels and seem to have a protective effect against some forms of cancer.

1¹/2 lbs salmon filet (preferably wild) cut into large bite-size pieces

¹/2 cup honey

¹/4 cup soy sauce

2 Tbsp lime or lemon juice

1 Tbsp finely grated ginger

sesame seeds, toasted, for sprinkling

Contents per stick

Calories	95
Total fat	2.4 g
saturated fat	0.6 g
monounsaturated fat	0.9 g
polyunsaturated fat	0.9 g
Protein	9.5 g
Carbohydrates	9.6 g
Cholesterol	24.6 mg
Fiber	0.0 g
Calories from fat	23%

1 Combine the honey, soy sauce, lime juice and ginger in a bowl or large zip-lock bag. Add the salmon and stir or shake to coat well. Cover (or seal) and refrigerate for 24 hours, or at least one hour if that's all you have time for.

2 When you're ready to cook them, thread each piece of salmon onto a bamboo skewer that has been soaked in water for at least 10 minutes. Grill over high heat for a couple minutes per side, until just cooked through, or broil for 3 - 4 minutes. Don't overcook or the salmon will dry out.

3 Place the sesame seeds in a shallow dish and dip one side of each skewer in the seeds to coat, or sprinkle them overtop. Serve immediately.

Makes about 18 salmon sticks.

Honey-Mustard Salmon Sticks
Add 1 Tbsp grainy Dijon mustard to the marinade mixture instead of the ginger.

Honey, Garlic & Ginger Sesame Chicken Sticks
Add 4 cloves of crushed garlic (and a small crumbled red chili pepper if you want more kick) to the marinade. Use skinless chicken breasts in place of the salmon. They'll take a little longer to cook.

Vietnamese Pork Meatballs

If you can get your hands on those little grassy bamboo serving picks, they look great with these meatballs. If you want to prep them in advance, freeze the raw meatballs on a cookie sheet and then transfer to a zip lock bag to store for up to 3 months. Place the frozen balls on a cookie sheet and pop them in the oven whenever you're ready for them.

1 lb lean ground pork

4 cloves garlic, crushed

2 stalks lemongrass

1 - 3 small red chilies, seeded

1 small bunch fresh cilantro

1 Tbsp packed brown sugar (optional)

1 Tbsp fish sauce (optional)

salt and pepper to taste

Contents per meatball

Calories	26
Total fat	0.5 g
saturated fat	0.2 g
monounsaturated fat	0.2 g
polyunsaturated fat	0.1 g
Protein	4.6 g
Carbohydrates	0.4 g
Cholesterol	11.2 mg
Fiber	0.0 g
Calories from fat	18%

1 Preheat oven to 350 F.

2 Remove the tough outer leaves of the lemongrass and finely chop the tender inner leaves. Finely chop the chilies and cilantro as well. Combine all the ingredients in a large bowl, mixing everything well with your hands.

3 Shape the mixture into balls and place about 1" apart on a rimmed baking sheet. Bake for 15 - 20 minutes, until cooked through. Alternately, you can heat a little sesame or canola oil in a non-stick sauté pan and cook the meatballs over medium heat for 5 - 10 minutes. I like to flatten them a little with my hand so you get more of the crunchy exterior on each one.

4 Serve plain or with any of the dipping sauces on page 127.

Makes about 2 dozen meatballs.

Cocktail Meatballs

I'm often introduced as a chef, but haven't been formally trained as one, and my love for these meatballs simmered in ketchup and grape jelly is evidence that I'm not. I am, however, the best eater I know. This is an old recipe my aunt used to make – if you like sticky sweet meaty things and haven't tried some version of cocktail meatballs yet, you must.

Meatballs

1/2 lb lean ground beef

1/2 lb ground chicken or turkey

1 small onion, grated

1 egg white

1 slice bread, processed into crumbs, or about 1/4 cup cracker crumbs

salt, pepper and garlic powder to taste

Sauce

1 cup ketchup or chili sauce, or 1/2 cup each

1 cup grape jelly

1/4 cup lemon juice

1 Preheat oven to 350 F.

2 Combine beef, chicken, onion, egg white, breadcrumbs, salt, pepper and garlic powder in a medium bowl.

3 Shape the mixture into small balls and place on a baking sheet. Bake for about 20 minutes, until cooked through.

4 In a medium saucepan combine the ketchup, jelly and lemon juice over medium heat. Cook, stirring often, until bubbly, and jelly has melted. Drop the meatballs into the sauce and simmer for 5 minutes, until heated through.

5 Serve in a chafing dish with toothpicks or in a fondue pot with fondue forks.

Makes about 2 dozen meatballs.

Contents per meatball

Calories	81
Total fat	1.4 g
saturated fat	0.6 g
monounsaturated fat	0.7 g
polyunsaturated fat	0.1 g
Protein	4.5 g
Carbohydrates	12.8 g
Cholesterol	10.8 mg
Fiber	0.4 g
Calories from fat	18%

Meatball Variations

Cocktail Sausages
Instead of making the meatballs, cook and slice a few lean chicken or turkey sausages and drop them into the sauce. Simmer until heated through.

Spicy Jelly Meatballs
Melt 1 cup peach, apricot or seedless raspberry jelly or jam with $1/4$ cup mustard and 1 Tbsp horseradish. Add meatballs or sausage and stir to coat.

Sweet Hoisin Meatballs
Combine $1/3$ cup each hoisin sauce and raspberry, currant or cranberry jelly, 1 clove crushed garlic, 1 tsp grated fresh ginger and 2 Tbsp water in a saucepan and bring to a simmer; add meatballs and stir to coat.

Sloppy Joe Meatballs
Combine a 14 oz can of tomato sauce, 2 Tbsp brown sugar, 1 Tbsp mustard, 1 tsp chili powder, $1/4$ tsp garlic salt and pepper and a few dashes of Tabasco sauce in a saucepan and bring to a simmer; add meatballs and simmer for 5 minutes, until heated through.

Good Things
in Small Packages

Wrapping food up in little packages makes it somehow more festive and special, even when it requires hardly any effort to prepare. The thrill of having something hiding inside, even if it's just cheesy filling, is not lost on adults.

Recipes with long instructions may seem daunting, but they are all a snap to make, even when they do require a little extra effort. It's a shame that cooking is so often portrayed as a chore; I find it to be a creative outlet, and one of the most gratifying and therapeutic ways to spend time. All cooks need eaters; in the end, the fact that homemade food is celebratory, comforting, nourishing and makes people happy is the best reward there is.

Curried Coconut Mango Chicken in Wonton Cups

Many people are under the impression that, because it comes from a plant, coconut milk contains healthy fat. Unfortunately, coconut milk is the exception to the rule – it contains 24 grams of fat per half cup, and it's virtually all saturated. An astonishing 91% of its calories come from fat! Light coconut milk is a much better choice, and if you want to boost the coconut flavor you can add a drop or two of coconut extract.

24 wonton wrappers

1 tsp canola oil

1 small onion, finely chopped

2 cloves garlic, crushed

1 Tbsp grated fresh ginger

2 cups shredded cooked chicken

1 Tbsp curry paste

1/2 cup light coconut milk

1/4 cup mango or peach chutney

juice of 1/2 a lime (about a tablespoon)

salt to taste

1 Tbsp chopped fresh cilantro (optional)

1 To make the wonton cups, press fresh wonton wrappers into mini muffin tins, pressing folds firmly to the sides, and bake at 350 F for 5 - 10 minutes, until pale golden. Set aside to cool.

2 To make the filling, heat oil in a medium non-stick saucepan and cook the onion, garlic and ginger for about 2 minutes. Add the chicken, curry paste, coconut milk, chutney, lime juice and salt. Cook, stirring often, until bubbly and thickened. Cool slightly or chill before spooning into wonton cups. Sprinkle with cilantro.

Makes 2 dozen cups.

Contents per wonton cup

Calories	69
Total fat	0.9 g
saturated fat	0.3 g
monounsaturated fat	0.3 g
polyunsaturated fat	0.3 g
Protein	7.1 g
Carbohydrates	7.3 g
Cholesterol	16.8 mg
Fiber	0.1 g
Calories from fat	13%

Samosas

Being little packages, samosas can be made with a variety of wrappings – you can buy naturally low-fat samosa wrappers fresh or frozen in ethnic grocery stores, or use phyllo pastry, fold into triangles and bake according to the directions on page 128. My friend and wonderful Indian cook, Tahera Rawji, taught me the easy, cheater's way to make samosas – using frozen hash browns! But feel free to boil, peel and chop potatoes to use in place of the hash browns if you like. Some people like to add a finely chopped jalapeno pepper to the filling too.

Filling

1 Tbsp canola oil

2 cloves garlic, crushed

1 Tbsp grated fresh ginger

1 tsp curry powder (optional)

1/2 tsp ground cumin

1/4 tsp ground coriander

1/4 tsp turmeric

1/4 tsp chili powder

3 cups frozen hash browns, thawed

1/2 cup frozen peas, thawed

1 tsp salt

1 Tbsp lemon juice

1 onion, finely chopped

1 Tbsp chopped fresh cilantro

1/2 tsp garam masala

Wraps

2 Tbsp flour

20 samosa wrappers

1 Tbsp canola oil

Contents per samosa

Calories	142
Total fat	2.9 g
saturated fat	0.3 g
monounsaturated fat	1.6 g
polyunsaturated fat	1.0 g
Protein	3.9 g
Carbohydrates	24.8 g
Cholesterol	1.4 mg
Fiber	1.4 g
Calories from fat	20%

1. In a large pan, heat oil over medium heat and add garlic, ginger, curry powder, cumin, coriander, turmeric and chili powder. Cook for a minute, then add the hash browns, peas, salt and lemon juice. Cook, stirring, for a few minutes, then remove from heat. Stir in the onion, cilantro and garam masala. Preheat oven to 350 F.

2. Put the flour in a small bowl and add enough water to make a paste. To assemble the samosas, put a spoonful of filling onto a samosa wrapper and fold into a triangle pocket, dipping your finger into the paste and using it to seal the edges and fill any little holes in the corners.

3. Place on a baking sheet and brush with the oil. Bake for 20 - 25 minutes, until golden. Serve with mango or peach chutney.

Makes 20 samosas.

Spinach & Potato Samosas

Replace the frozen peas with a few handfuls of fresh spinach, chopped. These are good with a minced jalapeno pepper thrown in as well.

Baked Spring Rolls

This is a great way to use up leftover roast chicken or pork, and if you have shrimp they're fantastic in place of the meat. For vegetarian rolls substitute tofu, rice noodles or more veggies. Spring roll wrappers vary in size – the ones I usually use are about 6" square – but you can use any size you like and adjust the baking time accordingly. These are great to pack for lunch, along with a few packets of plum sauce left over from takeout.

20 - 25 spring roll wrappers, thawed

3 cups finely shredded bok choy or sui choy

3 green onions, chopped

2 cups bean sprouts

1 large carrot, grated

10 dried shiitake mushrooms, soaked, drained and sliced (optional)

1 tsp salt

1/2 lb lean ground pork

1 tsp sesame oil

4 - 5 cloves garlic, crushed

1 Tbsp grated fresh ginger

canola oil for brushing

Contents per roll

Calories	237
Total fat	1.3 g
saturated fat	0.4 g
monounsaturated fat	0.4 g
polyunsaturated fat	0.5 g
Protein	13.0 g
Carbohydrates	41.9 g
Cholesterol	19.1 mg
Fiber	1.3 g
Calories from fat	7%

1. Preheat oven to 375 F.

2. In a large bowl, combine the bok choy, green onions, bean sprouts, carrot and mushrooms. Sprinkle with salt and toss to coat. Set aside.

3. In a medium skillet, cook pork with sesame oil, garlic and ginger until no longer pink. Set aside.

4. Take handfuls of the salted vegetables out of the bowl and squeeze out any excess liquid. Transfer to a dry bowl and add the pork mixture.

5. To make your spring rolls, lay one wrapper at a time on the counter with a point towards you, so it looks like a diamond. Keep the rest covered with a towel so they don't dry out. Spoon about 3 Tbsp of filling in a horizontal line just below the middle of the wrapper. Fold the bottom corner over the filling, roll over once, tuck in the ends and roll up like a cigar. Some wrappers will stick if you moisten the end, but most won't. That's OK – just place them seam side down on a cookie sheet and they'll hold together once they're baked. Brush with a little oil or spray with non-stick spray.

Top to bottom:
Chorizo Chipotle Dip
Tortilla Chips
Wonton Crisps
Edamamole

Clockwise from bottom:
Jelly Fauxnuts & Cheesecake Muffins
Berry, Peach, Apple or Plum Crumble Cake
Grape Focaccia
Cranberry Pecan Pumpkin Bread

Clockwise from bottom left:
Chewy Honey Roasted Nut & Seed Clusters
Peanut Butter & Honey Gorp
Pizza Pretzels
Hot Soft Pretzels
Spicy Cheese Fries

Left to right:
Curried Coconut Mango Chicken in Wonton Cups
Potstickers
Hoisin Chicken Lettuce Wraps

Greek Mini Pita Pockets

You can put together a platter of these pockets in less time than it takes to order a pizza, and they make perfect in-front-of-the-TV food. Fill full sized pita breads to pack for lunch.

6 Bake for 20 minutes, until golden and crispy. Serve with Sesame or Peanut Plum Sauce (recipes below) or bottled plum sauce.

Makes about 20 spring rolls.

Sesame Plum Sauce

Stir together 1/2 cup plum sauce, 1/4 cup soy sauce, 2 Tbsp rice vinegar and 1/2 tsp sesame oil. If you like, stir in a spoonful of sesame seeds too.

Peanut Plum Sauce

Stir together 1/4 cup plum sauce, 1/4 cup water, 2 Tbsp peanut butter, 1 Tbsp lime juice, 1 1/2 tsp fish sauce, 1/2 tsp grated fresh ginger and 1/2 tsp chili paste.

12 mini pita breads, white or whole wheat

2 cups shredded roasted chicken or lamb, or lamb kebabs (page 114)

1/2 cup crumbled feta or paneer cheese

thinly sliced purple onion

chopped tomato

shredded lettuce

1 cup tzatziki or hummus (pages 66 and 70)

1 Gently warm the pita breads and split them in half across the middle, forming two pockets. Stuff them with chicken, cheese, onion, tomato, lettuce and tzatziki.

2 Stack them on a platter or fold each one into a small cocktail napkin to serve.

Makes 24.

Contents per pita (with tzatziki)

Calories	67
Total fat	0.6 g
saturated fat	0.2 g
monounsaturated fat	0.2 g
polyunsaturated fat	0.2 g
Protein	7.7 g
Carbohydrates	6.8 g
Cholesterol	16.7 mg
Fiber	0.3 g
Calories from fat	11%

Curried Chicken Salad Mini Pita Pockets

My favorite food writer, Laurie Colwin, once likened chicken salad to a little black dress: it can be dressed up or down to suit any occasion. My Mom likes it with tuna instead of chicken.

12 mini pita breads, white or whole wheat

2 cups shredded roasted chicken

2 stalks celery, finely chopped

2 green onions, finely chopped

1 tart apple, finely chopped

1/4 cup chopped raisins OR
1/2 cup halved grapes

1/3 cup light mayonnaise

1 tsp lemon juice

1/2 tsp grated fresh ginger

1/2 tsp curry paste or powder

pinch of salt, pepper and cumin

1 Split the pitas in half across the middle, forming two pockets. Mix all the remaining ingredients and stuff the pitas, adding a little shredded lettuce if you like.

2 Stack them on a platter or fold each one into a cocktail napkin to serve.

Makes 24.

Contents per pita

Calories	71
Total fat	1.2 g
saturated fat	0.2 g
monounsaturated fat	0.6 g
polyunsaturated fat	0.4 g
Protein	7.1 g
Carbohydrates	7.4 g
Cholesterol	16.1 mg
Fiber	0.5 g
Calories from fat	18%

Vietnamese Rice Paper Rolls

Also called Summer Rolls, rice paper rolls are wonderful to learn how to make. They're cheap, portable, perfect to bring to a party or for lunch, and very low in fat and calories. Rolling them is easier than you might think. Stuff them with anything you like – thinly sliced red pepper, pea pods, lettuce, crab, blanched asparagus, bean sprouts, chives, jicama and mango are all delicious. They are fantastic made with shreds of leftover cooked chicken or pork in place of the shrimp, or leave out the meat altogether for vegetarian rolls. They make a great dinner when it's too hot to cook. All the filling measurements below are approximate.

15 rice paper wrappers

Filling
100g (3½ oz) thin rice vermicelli noodles (about a handful)

1 Tbsp rice vinegar

1 large carrot, peeled and shredded

15 cooked shrimp, peeled and deveined

½ cucumber, peeled if necessary and cut into thin sticks

small handful fresh cilantro, mint or thai basil leaves, torn up or left whole

½ cup chopped peanuts (optional)

Ginger Mango Dipping Sauce
Combine ½ cup mango chutney, 2 Tbsp water, 2 Tbsp rice wine vinegar, the juice of 1 lime and 1 tsp grated fresh ginger.

Sweet Lime Dipping Sauce
Combine 2 Tbsp each lime juice and fish sauce and 1 Tbsp each brown sugar and water.

Garlic Dipping Sauce
Combine 3 Tbsp fish sauce, 2 cloves crushed garlic and 2 Tbsp honey.

Nuoc Cham
Combine ¼ cup each rice vinegar and fish sauce, 2 Tbsp lime juice, 3 Tbsp sugar, 3 cloves crushed garlic and 1 fresh hot Asian chili or jalapeno pepper, seeded and finely chopped.

1. To prepare the filling, place noodles in a bowl of boiling water and let stand for about 3 minutes (or as package directs) to soften. Drain well and place in a medium bowl. Add carrot and rice vinegar and toss to combine. Cut the shrimp lengthwise in half.

2. To assemble the rolls, fill a shallow dish (I use a pie plate) with hot water and lay a clean tea towel over your work surface. Soak one rice paper round at a time in the water for about 10 seconds, until it's pliable, and lay it on the tea towel. Pat the surface with the edges of the towel to absorb any excess water.

3. Place two shrimp halves (cut side up so you can see the pink through the wrapper), a stick of cucumber and some noodles down the middle of the round. Sprinkle with cilantro and peanuts. Fold over one long side to cover, then fold up both ends. Roll the whole thing up as tightly as you can without tearing the wrapper.

4. Serve with peanut sauce (see page 109) or any of the dipping sauces on this page.

Makes 15 rolls.

Spanakopita (Spinach & Feta) Triangles

"Phyllo" is the Greek word for "leaf", and refers to thinner-than-paper pastry sheets made of flour and water. Phyllo pastry contains almost no fat on its own, but becomes very high in fat when each layer is slathered with butter. Many low-fat recipes call for non-stick spray to be sprayed between the layers, but that doesn't add any flavor! I prefer to brush sparingly with real butter or olive oil instead. If you want to add extra crunch, sprinkle dry bread crumbs or Parmesan cheese between the layers.

12 sheets phyllo pastry

1/4 cup melted butter, canola or olive oil, or a combination

Filling

1 tsp canola oil

1 onion, finely chopped

2 cloves garlic, crushed

1 - 10 oz package frozen chopped spinach, thawed and drained

1 cup crumbled feta cheese (about 4 oz)

2 egg whites

salt and pepper to taste

chopped fresh dill or mint (optional)

Contents per triangle

Calories	131
Total fat	7.1 g
saturated fat	4.1 g
monounsaturated fat	2.0 g
polyunsaturated fat	1.0 g
Protein	4.1 g
Carbohydrates	12.0 g
Cholesterol	19.0 mg
Fiber	0.7 g
Calories from fat	51%

1 In a medium sauté pan, cook onion and garlic in oil until soft. Add spinach and cook until moisture has evaporated. Transfer to a bowl and cool slightly. Stir in feta, egg whites, salt and pepper and some fresh dill or mint if you like.

2 Preheat oven to 400 F.

3 Take two sheets of phyllo and stack them on a clean work surface; cover the rest with a tea towel so it doesn't dry out. Brush the first sheet of phyllo very lightly with butter and top with the second sheet. (A trick I use to apply the butter sparingly is to dip the brush in warm water, then squeeze it out well with my fingers. That way when I dip it into the butter it only sits on the surface, rather than saturating the bristles with butter.)

4 Cut the sheet in half lengthwise and then again into quarters so you have 4 long strips. Place a spoonful of filling at one end of each strip and fold the corner over it diagonally. Continue folding the strip as if you were folding a flag, maintaining the triangle shape.

5 Place the packets seam side down on a cookie sheet. (They can be prepared up to this point and frozen in a single layer and then transferred to a plastic

Curried Chicken Phyllo Triangles

Phyllo dries out quickly and tears easily, but it is really very forgiving – because there are so many flaky layers, it's easy to patch a tear or simply layer over it. No one will ever know!

bag. Pop them out of the freezer and bake them from frozen.)

6 If there is any butter left use it to brush the tops of the triangles, or spray them with some non-stick spray. Bake for 15 - 20 minutes, until golden.

Makes 2 dozen triangles.

Chicken, Spinach, Sun-dried Tomato and Feta Triangles

Add 1/2 cup chopped cooked chicken and 1/4 cup chopped sun-dried tomatoes (packed in oil or soaked in water) to the spinach mixture.

8 sheets phyllo pastry

1/4 cup melted butter, canola or olive oil, or a combination

Filling

1 Tbsp butter

1 small onion, finely chopped

1 Tbsp flour

1 tsp curry powder

salt and pepper to taste

1/2 cup milk

2 cups chopped cooked chicken

1/4 cup sliced or slivered almonds, toasted

1/4 cup currants or golden raisins

Grated zest of 1 orange (optional)

To make the filling:

1 In a medium saucepan, sauté onion in butter until soft. Add the flour, curry powder, salt and pepper and cook, stirring, for 1 minute. Add the milk and cook for a few minutes, until it's bubbly and thickened. Stir in the chicken, almonds, raisins and orange zest. If it's too thick to stir, add a little splash of milk. Set aside until it's cool enough to handle.

2 Fill the phyllo and bake according to the directions for Spanakopita.

Makes 16 triangles.

Contents per Curried Chicken Phyllo Triangle ▶	
Calories	128
Total fat	5.7 g
saturated fat	2.7 g
monounsaturated fat	2.1 g
polyunsaturated fat	0.9 g
Protein	10.9 g
Carbohydrates	6.9 g
Cholesterol	34.0 mg
Fiber	0.4 g
Calories from fat	44%

Hoisin Chicken Lettuce Wraps

Lettuce wraps were in fashion far before Dr. Atkins encouraged us to forgo bread in favor of greens as a sandwich casing. This recipe is dead easy to make and very stylish to serve on a platter with wedges of iceberg lettuce; your friends scoop filling onto a lettuce leaf, wrap and eat. Lettuce wraps are substantial enough to make a meal, and perfect to serve at a party or put out on the Scrabble table. Use button mushrooms instead of shiitake if you like.

1 Tbsp canola or sesame oil

1 lb skinless, boneless chicken breast, chopped into small strips

2 cups fresh shiitake mushrooms, sliced (about 4 or 5 mushrooms)

3 cloves garlic, crushed

1 Tbsp grated fresh ginger

salt and pepper to taste

1 small red pepper, seeded and finely chopped

1/2 can water chestnuts, drained and chopped (optional)

3 green onions, chopped

1/4 cup hoisin sauce

1/2 large head iceberg lettuce, quartered

1. Heat the oil in a large non-stick skillet and cook the chicken over medium-high heat for a few minutes, until opaque. Add the mushrooms and cook for another minute or two, until they are starting to turn golden. Add the garlic, ginger, salt and pepper and cook a minute more. Add the red pepper, water chestnuts and green onions. Cook for another minute.

2. Add the hoisin sauce and toss to coat well and heat through. Transfer the chicken mixture to a serving platter and serve alongside the wedges of iceberg lettuce. To eat, pile some of the chicken mixture onto a lettuce leaf, wrap it up and eat it like a burrito.

Makes about 16 wraps.

Curried Tuna Lettuce Wraps
Stir together a can of tuna, 1 Tbsp lemon juice, a finely chopped rib of celery, 1/4 cup light mayonnaise, 1 tsp curry powder, 1 cup halved seedless grapes and salt and pepper to taste. Serve alongside wedges of iceberg lettuce.

Contents per wrap

Calories	54
Total fat	1.2 g
saturated fat	0.2 g
monounsaturated fat	0.6 g
polyunsaturated fat	0.4 g
Protein	7.5 g
Carbohydrates	3.1 g
Cholesterol	16.4 mg
Fiber	0.5 g
Calories from fat	22%

Three Cheese Caramelized Onion, Spinach & Mushroom Calzone

A calzone is just a folded-in-half pizza, like a real pizza pocket. They can be filled with anything you'd use to top a pizza. You can freeze them unbaked, and bake frozen or freeze them after you bake them. Take them to work and by lunchtime they're thawed enough to pop in the microwave and warm up.

1 batch pizza dough (see page 92)

1 tsp canola oil

1 onion, cut in half and thinly sliced

2 cups sliced mushrooms

2 cloves garlic, crushed

1 - 10 oz package frozen chopped spinach, thawed

1 cup part skim ricotta cheese

1 egg

salt and pepper to taste

1/2 cup grated mozzarella cheese

1/4 cup grated Parmesan cheese

Contents per calzone

Calories	525
Total fat	11.5 g
saturated fat	5.7 g
monounsaturated fat	4.2 g
polyunsaturated fat	1.6 g
Protein	25.5 g
Carbohydrates	77.1 g
Cholesterol	81.8 mg
Fiber	5.8 g
Calories from fat	22%

1 Preheat oven to 450 F.

2 In a large non-stick skillet, sauté the onions in the oil over medium-low heat until golden. Transfer to a medium bowl and set aside. In the same skillet, sauté the mushrooms and garlic for 3 minutes, until browned. Squeeze as much water as possible out of the spinach and add to the mushrooms; cook until the moisture is gone. Set aside to cool slightly.

3 Add the ricotta, egg, salt and pepper, spinach mixture, mozzarella and Parmesan to the onions and stir until well blended.

4 Divide the pizza dough into 4 balls and roll each out into a 7"- 8" circle. Divide the mushroom mixture between the circles, leaving at least a 1/2" border around the edge. Fold the dough over the filling and press together to seal. If you like, crimp the edge with your fingers or a fork. Transfer to an ungreased cookie sheet and cut a couple small slashes in the top to let the steam escape. You can brush the tops with a little beaten egg to give them a shiny finish.

5 Bake for 10 minutes, then reduce the oven temperature to 350 F and bake for another 20 minutes, until golden.

Makes 4 calzone.

Stromboli

Besides being a volcano on one of the Aeolian Islands of Italy, a stromboli is also a rolled-up pizza-like sandwich you can hold in your hand. A whole stromboli is a meal in itself, or you can slice them thickly and serve as two-bite snacks.

1 batch pizza dough (see page 92)

¼ cup grated Parmesan cheese

12 slices Black Forest or
honey ham (about 100 g)

12 slices thinly sliced Provolone or
mozzarella cheese (about 150 g)

1 - 2 roasted red peppers (see page 73),
chopped

1 egg, lightly beaten

Contents per stromboli

Calories	348
Total fat	7.7 g
saturated fat	4.1 g
monounsaturated fat	2.8 g
polyunsaturated fat	0.8 g
Protein	18.9 g
Carbohydrates	47.8 g
Cholesterol	62 mg
Fiber	2.5 g
Calories from fat	22%

1 Preheat oven to 400 F.

2 Divide the dough into 6 pieces and roll each into an 8" circle on a lightly floured surface. Sprinkle each piece with Parmesan cheese and layer with ham, provolone and red peppers.

3 Roll the dough up, folding the ends over and pinching them to seal. Place the rolls on a cookie sheet and brush with the beaten egg. Cut a few small vents in each roll to let the steam out.

4 Bake for about 30 minutes, until golden. Let cool slightly before serving.

Makes 6 stromboli.

Mushroom & Onion Stromboli
Sauté a thinly sliced onion and 2 cups sliced mushrooms in a little oil until golden. Use in place of the ham, and bake as directed.

Stuffed Pizza Bites with Saucy Dip

Bite-sized pizza is perfect for little fingers, especially when the filling is enclosed within the crust. These are great to put out on the table when you're watching a movie. Pepperoni is intensely flavored so you don't need to use much, but you could also use ham, mushrooms, chopped roasted red pepper... anything that goes onto pizza works in a pizza bite.

1 can refrigerated breadstick dough (such as Pillsbury)

1 pepperoni stick, cut into 24 slices

3 - 1/4" slices part skim mozzarella cheese, cut into cubes (about 90 g)

1/4 tsp dried Italian seasoning or oregano

1 Tbsp grated Parmesan cheese

1 cup spaghetti or pizza sauce for dipping

Contents per pizza bite

Calories	64
Total fat	1.8 g
saturated fat	0.9 g
monounsaturated fat	0.8 g
polyunsaturated fat	0.1 g
Protein	2.8 g
Carbohydrates	6.9 g
Cholesterol	4.4 mg
Fiber	0.1 g
Calories from fat	38%

1 Preheat oven to 375 F.

2 Unroll the dough and separate it into 8 breadsticks. Cut each one crosswise into thirds to make 24 pieces. Flatten each until it is 1" - 1 1/2" wide.

3 Place a piece of pepperoni and a square of cheese in the middle of each piece of dough and fold over the ends to enclose them, pressing the edges to seal. Place seam side down on a cookie sheet.

4 Sprinkle the bundles with Italian seasoning and Parmesan cheese. Bake for 15 - 20 minutes, until golden. Serve immediately. Warm up the spaghetti sauce and serve alongside for dipping.

Makes 24 bites.

Jalapeño Poppers

The first time I tasted these in a pub they were just this side of awful, and I've been determined to make them the way I think they ought to taste ever since. Although I'm a wimp when it comes to spice, I'm a sucker for anything gooey and cheesy, and I was pleasantly surprised at how mild the peppers taste once baked – almost like green bell peppers, with a little more kick.

6 good-sized fresh jalapeno peppers

1/2 - 8 oz (250 g) package light cream cheese, softened

1/2 cup grated part skim mozzarella, cheddar or Monterey Jack cheese

1/2 tsp ground cumin (optional)

pinch cayenne (optional)

2 large eggs

1/2 cup flour

1/2 tsp garlic powder

1/4 tsp each salt and pepper

1 - 2 cups panko (crunchy Japanese breadcrumbs), or fine dry breadcrumbs

1/2 tsp paprika

Contents per popper

Calories	87
Total fat	3.2 g
saturated fat	1.7 g
monounsaturated fat	1.2 g
polyunsaturated fat	0.3 g
Protein	4.0 g
Carbohydrates	9.5 g
Cholesterol	43.2 mg
Fiber	0.5 g
Calories from fat	37%

1 Preheat the oven to 350 F.

2 Cut the jalapeños in half lengthwise and remove the seeds and membranes.

3 In a small bowl, stir together the cream cheese, mozzarella, cumin and cayenne if you're using it. Stuff the jalapeño halves with the cheese mixture – they will be overflowing! That's OK. (When I do this, I take a bit of cheese in my hand and roll it into a cylinder, then press it into the pepper.)

4 Get three shallow bowls. In one, beat the eggs with a fork. In another, combine the flour, garlic powder, salt and pepper. In the third combine the crumbs and paprika.

5 One at a time, dredge the jalapeños in flour, then in the beaten egg, and then into the crumbs, pressing to coat well. Place the coated peppers, cut side up, on a baking sheet that has been sprayed with non-stick spray.

6 Bake for about 30 minutes, until golden and bubbly. Serve immediately.

Makes 12 poppers.

Salsa Poppers
Stir 1/4 cup salsa into the cheese mixture before stuffing the peppers.

Tuna Stuffed Tomatoes

You know the saying 'life is too short to stuff mushrooms'? I disagree... if the payoff justifies the effort! These require a little more prep than most of the recipes in this book but they are really quite yummy, and if you are like me and like to cook you may even enjoy it. If you have extra little hands in the house, they usually like to help fill the tomatoes. These make perfect tea party fare, and are great to keep in the fridge for snacking.

1 can tuna in water, drained

1/2 - 8 oz (250 g) tub light cream cheese

1 ripe avocado

1 Tbsp lemon juice

1/4 tsp chili powder (optional)

1/2 tsp Worcestershire sauce

few shakes Tabasco sauce (optional)

salt and pepper to taste

2 pints cherry tomatoes

1 Mash everything but the tomatoes together in a bowl.

2 Cut a thin slice off the tops of the tomatoes and hollow out the centers. If you are cooking for a party, turn them upside-down to drain on paper towels. Fill each tomato with the tuna and cream cheese mixture. Chill until ready to serve.

Makes about 4 dozen.

Contents per tomato

Calories	18
Total fat	1.1 g
saturated fat	0.4 g
monounsaturated fat	0.6 g
polyunsaturated fat	0.1 g
Protein	1.1 g
Carbohydrates	1.0 g
Cholesterol	2.3 mg
Fiber	0.3 g
Calories from fat	56%

Potstickers

When I make potstickers, I make a large batch and freeze half to throw into simmering chicken broth for fast wonton soup. You can find square or round wonton wrappers fresh or frozen in Asian markets and most grocery stores. If the pre-ground pork at the grocery store seems too fatty, buy pork tenderloin, chop it and pulse in your food processor until it's ground.

1 cup finely shredded bok choy or napa cabbage

1/2 tsp salt

1/2 lb lean ground pork

1 cup thinly sliced mushrooms

2 green onions, finely chopped

1 Tbsp soy sauce

1-2 cloves garlic, crushed

1 tsp grated fresh ginger

1/2 tsp sugar

1 tsp sesame oil

1 package wonton wrappers (about 30)

1 Tbsp canola oil

Chicken stock or water

Garlic Chili Dipping Sauce

1/2 cup soy sauce

2 Tbsp packed brown sugar

2 Tbsp rice vinegar

2 Tbsp lime or lemon juice

1 tsp sesame oil

2 cloves garlic, crushed

1 green onion, chopped

1 tsp chilli sauce or sambal olek

1. In a medium bowl, toss the cabbage with salt and let stand for 5 minutes. Pick it up in your hand and squeeze out the excess liquid, draining it as well as you can. Add the pork, mushrooms, green onions, soy sauce, garlic, ginger, sugar and sesame oil and mix it all up with your hands.

2. To fill wontons, place a small spoonful of filling in the middle of each wrapper; moisten the edges with water (just use your finger) and fold over, pressing the edge tightly to seal. Place seam side up on a cookie sheet, pressing lightly to flatten the bottom. Cover with a tea towel to prevent them from drying out. (Dumplings can be prepared up to this point, covered with plastic wrap, and refrigerated for up to 24 hours, or frozen.)

3. When you're ready to cook the potstickers, heat 1/2 Tbsp canola oil in a large skillet over medium-high heat. Place half the dumplings at a time in the skillet and cook for a minute or two, until deep golden brown on the bottom, shaking the pan a few times to keep them from sticking. Don't crowd the pan too much.

Potsticker Variations

There are endless variations on Potstickers. Here are just a few.

4 Pour about $1/3$ cup stock or water into the pan. Cover, reduce heat to medium and cook for about 5 minutes – this will allow them to steam. Uncover and cook until the bottoms of the dumplings are very crisp and the liquid has evaporated, about 5 - 7 more minutes.

5 To make the garlic-chili dipping sauce, mix all the ingredients together in a bowl or shake them all up in a jar. Remove the potstickers from the pan and serve immediately with garlic-chili dipping sauce, or spike some soy sauce with a little sesame oil and rice wine vinegar. To fancy it up, add a chopped green onion and some grated fresh ginger and/or garlic.

Makes 2 - $2^1/2$ dozen potstickers.

Contents per potsticker

Calories	45
Total fat	0.9 g
saturated fat	0.2 g
monounsaturated fat	0.4 g
polyunsaturated fat	0.3 g
Protein	3.0 g
Carbohydrates	5.9 g
Cholesterol	5.2 mg
Fiber	0.4 g
Calories from fat	20%

Other potsticker fillings to try:

• finely chop 1 Tbsp minced fresh ginger, 2 cloves garlic, 1 cup chopped, blanched fresh asparagus, 1 can water chestnuts, drained, 3 green onions, 1 tsp sesame oil and 1 tsp soy sauce in a food processor. Stir in some finely chopped leftover roast duck if you like.

• 1 lb crabmeat, 1 egg white, 1 Tbsp rice vinegar, 1 Tbsp grated fresh ginger, 1 tsp sesame oil, and 2 Tbsp chopped fresh cilantro.

• $1/4$ lb each ground pork and uncooked shrimp, shelled, deveined, and finely chopped, 1 egg white, $1/4$ cup finely chopped water chestnuts, 1 Tbsp chopped fresh cilantro, 1 tsp grated fresh ginger, $1/2$ tsp each sugar, salt and sesame oil.

• blanch a packed cup of spinach in simmering water for a few seconds, until wilted. Rinse under cold water, squeeze out as much moisture as possible and chop finely. Stir in 6 oz shelled, deveined, and chopped shrimp, $1/4$ cup finely chopped water chestnuts, 2 finely chopped green onions, 1 tsp sesame oil, 2 tsp grated fresh ginger, 1 tsp sugar and $1/2$ tsp salt.

Chicken Negimaki

Chicken negimaki sounds complicated, but it's really not. It's tasty and elegant enough for a party. If you don't have a mallet, use a can or bottle to pound the chicken. If you don't have kitchen string, use dental floss – just not the minty kind!

3 chicken breast halves,
without the tenders (about 1^1/2 lbs)

1 bunch green onions

^{1}/4 cup soy sauce

2 Tbsp rice vinegar

2 tsp sesame oil

1 - 2 cloves garlic, crushed

sesame seeds for rolling (optional)

1 tsp canola or sesame oil

Contents per piece

Calories	33
Total fat	0.6 g
saturated fat	0.1 g
monounsaturated fat	0.3 g
polyunsaturated fat	0.2 g
Protein	5.4 g
Carbohydrates	0.9 g
Cholesterol	12.2 mg
Fiber	0.2 g
Calories from fat	22%

1. Place the chicken breasts between 2 pieces of plastic wrap and pound them until they are about ^{1}/2" thick. Place them smooth side down with a long side toward you and lay two green onions along the middle. Roll the chicken around the onions and tie with kitchen string or dental floss to hold them together.

2. In a shallow dish, stir together the soy sauce, vinegar, sesame oil and garlic. Marinate the negimaki rolls for at least a few hours or up to 24 hours.

3. When you're ready to cook the negimaki, spread sesame seeds on a cookie sheet. Remove the negimaki from the marinade and roll them in sesame seeds to coat. Heat canola oil in a large non-stick skillet and cook the rolls over medium heat for about 10 minutes, turning them until they're cooked through.

4. Transfer to a cutting board and cut into 1" thick slices. If you like, these can be served on bamboo skewers. Serve with Sweet Red Pepper Dip on the following page.

Makes about 30 negimaki.

Sweet Red Pepper Dip

Visually, this bright red dip is gorgeous. Although it's made to go with Chicken Negimaki, try it with Vietnamese Pork Meatballs (see page 117) or Vietnamese Rice Paper Rolls (see page 127).

1 small red bell pepper, seeded and chopped

1/2 cup white vinegar

1/3 cup sugar

pinch dried red pepper flakes

salt to taste

1 To make the red pepper dip, pulse the red pepper and vinegar in a food processor until pureed.

2 Transfer to a saucepan and add the sugar, red pepper flakes and salt. Bring to a simmer and cook for 5 minutes; set aside to cool. Serve at room temperature or chilled.

Make about 1¹/2 cups.

Contents per Tbsp

Calories	13
Total fat	0 g
Protein	0.1 g
Carbohydrates	3.5 g
Cholesterol	0.0 mg
Fiber	0.1 g
Calories from fat	0%

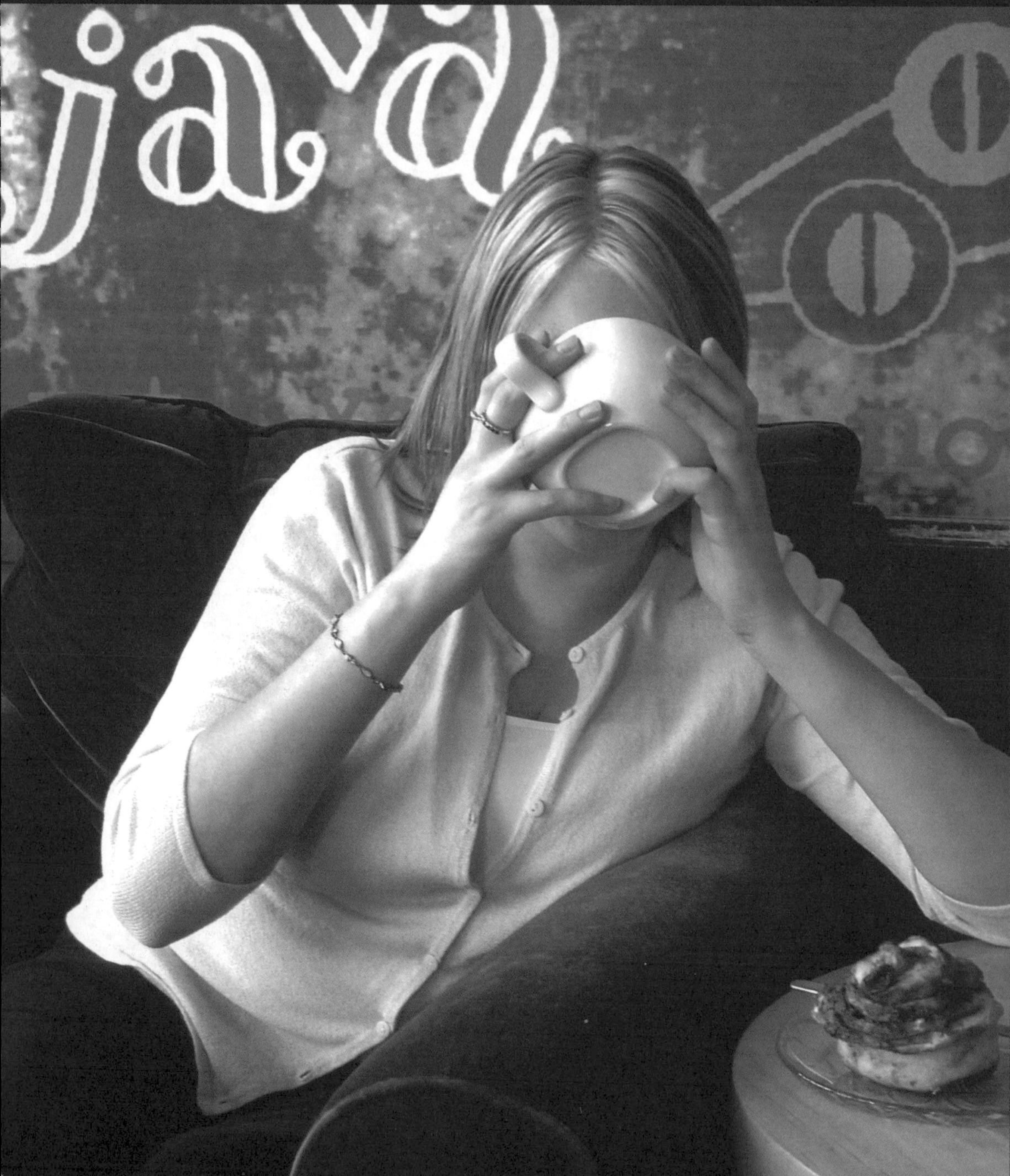

Lovin' from the Oven

Home cooks seem to be divided into two camps: there are bakers and there are chefs. Some love to bake, and others prefer to cook meals. For me, the act of baking itself is as addictive and satisfying as the end result. Unfortunately home baking is also the ultimate test of self control, so it's best to only bake when there are other people around to save you from yourself. This is why people who bake also tend to make a lot of friends.

When I was about 7 I started the Kooky Cupcake Company, took out a loan for $20 from my Mum for ingredients, and in the end (after paying back my loan) profited about $14 selling cupcakes up and down our alley. (A lot of the profits were, um, eaten up.)

Berry Whole Wheat White Chocolate Drop Scones

After spending a small fortune on raspberry whole wheat scones at Starbucks I decided to develop a recipe myself, and have acquired a few new friends as a result. If you use frozen berries – and you can use any kind you like – leave them frozen rather than thawing them before you stir them in. Drop scones are easy, but if you want a sturdier dough that you can cut into rounds or wedges, use only 3/4 cup milk.

1 1/2 cups whole wheat flour

1 cup flour

1/2 cup sugar

1 Tbsp baking powder

1/2 tsp salt

1/4 cup butter or margarine

1 cup milk

1 large egg

1 cup fresh or frozen (unthawed) raspberries, blackberries or blueberries

1/2 cup chopped white chocolate

Contents per scone

Calories	209
Total fat	6.4 g
saturated fat	3.9 g
monounsaturated fat	2.0 g
polyunsaturated fat	0.5 g
Protein	4.7 g
Carbohydrates	33.8 g
Cholesterol	29.1 mg
Fiber	3.1 g
Calories from fat	29%

1. Preheat oven to 400 F.

2. In a large bowl combine flours, sugar, baking powder and salt. Cut in the butter until well blended and crumbly. In a small bowl stir together the milk and egg; add to the flour mixture. Stir until almost blended, then add the berries and chocolate and stir gently just until the mixture is combined.

3. Drop large spoonfuls of dough onto a cookie sheet that has been sprayed with non-stick spray. (If you make thicker dough, turn it out onto a lightly floured surface and pat into a circle about 1/2" thick, then cut into wedges with a knife or into rounds with a cookie cutter or glass rim.) Sprinkle the tops with a little sugar if you want.

4. Bake for 20 - 25 minutes, until golden. Serve warm.

Makes 12 scones.

Blueberry Lemon Drop Scones
Add the grated zest of 1 lemon to the milk mixture, and use fresh or frozen blueberries instead of the raspberries.

Cranberry Orange Drop Scones
Add the grated zest of 1 orange to the milk mixture, and use fresh or frozen cranberries instead of the raspberries.

Dried Fruit & Nut Scones

I wake up every Sunday morning craving freshly baked scones! When you bake with dried fruit, make sure it's plump – fruit that's too dried out will absorb too much moisture from whatever batter you stir them into. If you want to boost the fiber, use half whole wheat flour.

3 cups flour

1/3 cup sugar

1 Tbsp baking powder

1/2 tsp baking soda

1/4 tsp salt

grated zest of 1 orange

1/4 cup butter or stick margarine

1/2 cup dried fruit, such as cranberries, raisins, chopped apricots or cherries

1/4 cup chopped pecans or walnuts (optional)

3/4 cup buttermilk

1 large egg

1 large apple, coarsely grated

Contents per scone

Calories	210
Total fat	4.4 g
saturated fat	2.7 g
monounsaturated fat	1.3 g
polyunsaturated fat	0.4 g
Protein	4.6 g
Carbohydrates	37.6 g
Cholesterol	18.8 mg
Fiber	1.7 g
Calories from fat	20%

1. Preheat oven to 400 F.

2. In a large bowl, combine the flour, sugar, baking powder, baking soda, salt and orange zest. Using a pastry blender, whisk or fork, add the butter and work it in until the mixture is well blended and crumbly. Stir in the dried fruit and nuts.

3. In a small bowl, stir together the buttermilk and egg. Add to the flour mixture along with the grated apple and stir just until you have a soft dough. On a lightly floured surface, pat the dough about 3/4" thick and cut into rounds with a biscuit cutter, glass rim or the open end of a can.

4. Place on a cookie sheet that has been sprayed with non-stick spray. If you like, brush the tops with a little milk and sprinkle with sugar. Bake for 15 - 20 minutes, until golden.

Makes 12 scones.

Whole Wheat Banana Walnut Scones
Use half whole wheat flour and half all-purpose flour, omit the dried fruit, replace the grated apple with 2 mashed ripe bananas, and include walnuts.

Banana Bread

Everyone needs a good banana bread recipe in their repertoire. I love making peanut butter sandwiches on banana bread, or toasting a slice and spreading it with cream cheese. To make muffins instead of a loaf, divide the batter among 12 muffin tins that have been sprayed with non-stick spray or lined with paper liners. Bake at 400 F for 20 - 25 minutes, until golden and springy to the touch.

1/4 cup butter or margarine, softened

3/4 cup sugar

1 1/2 cups mashed very ripe banana (about 3 bananas)

2 large eggs

1/3 cup plain low fat yogurt, low fat sour cream or buttermilk

1 tsp vanilla

2 cups flour, or half all purpose and half whole wheat flour

1 tsp baking soda

1/2 tsp salt

1/3 cup chopped walnuts, pecans or chocolate or butterscotch chips (optional)

OR 1 cup fresh or frozen (unthawed) blueberries (optional)

1 Preheat oven to 350 F.

2 In a large bowl, beat butter and sugar until well combined – the mixture will have the consistency of wet sand. Add banana, eggs, yogurt and vanilla and beat until well blended. Don't worry about getting all the lumps of banana out.

3 Add flour, baking soda and salt and stir by hand just until combined. If you are adding nuts or other additions, throw them in just before it's blended.

4 Pour batter into an 8" x 4" loaf pan that has been sprayed with non-stick spray. Bake for an hour and ten minutes, until the top is springy to the touch. Cool in the pan on a wire rack.

Makes one loaf, about 16 slices.

Chocolate Swirl Banana Bread
Remove 1 cup of batter and gently stir 2 Tbsp cocoa and 1/4 cup chocolate chips into it. Alternate big spoonfuls of plain and chocolate batter in the pan and gently run a knife through to create a marbled effect. Bake as directed.

Lemon Banana Bread
Add the grated zest of 1 lemon to the butter and sugar mixture. Brush the warm loaf with a glaze made of 1/4 cup icing sugar and 1 Tbsp lemon juice.

Contents per slice

Calories	152
Total fat	3.5 g
saturated fat	2.1 g
monounsaturated fat	1.1 g
polyunsaturated fat	0.3 g
Protein	2.9 g
Carbohydrates	26.8 g
Cholesterol	35 mg
Fiber	0.8 g
Calories from fat	22%

Apple Muesli Bread

This sturdy and wholesome bread is the perfect vehicle for peanut butter or cream cheese, but is just as good plain. Use any assortment of dried fruit, nuts and seeds, or try adding fresh or frozen berries. To make muffins instead of a loaf, divide the batter among 12 muffin tins that have been sprayed with non-stick spray or lined with paper liners. Bake at 400 F for 20 - 25 minutes, until golden and springy to the touch.

1^1/$_2$ cups flour

1^1/$_2$ cups whole wheat flour

3/4 cup sugar

1 Tbsp baking powder

^{1}/$_2$ tsp salt

1^1/$_2$ cups milk

^{1}/$_4$ cup canola oil or melted butter

1 large egg

1 grated apple, peeled or unpeeled

^{1}/$_2$ cup dried fruit, such as raisins, cranberries and chopped apricots

^{1}/$_2$ cup coarsely chopped nuts (pecans, walnuts, almonds, hazelnuts or a combination)

1 Tbsp oats

1 Preheat oven to 350 F.

2 In a large bowl, combine flours, sugar, baking powder and salt. In a small bowl, whisk together the milk, oil and egg.

3 Make a well in the dry ingredients and add the milk mixture along with the apple. Stir a few strokes, then add the dried fruit and nuts and stir just until combined.

4 Spread into a 9" x 5" loaf pan that has been sprayed with non-stick spray, and sprinkle oats over the top. Bake for one hour, until the top is cracked and golden and the loaf is springy to the touch. Cool in the pan on a wire rack.

Makes 1 loaf, with about 16 slices.

Whole Wheat Berry Bread
Replace the dried fruit with fresh or frozen berries and add the grated zest of a lemon.

Whole Wheat Nut Bread
Omit the apple and dried fruit and increase the nuts to 1 cup. This loaf is a great source of healthy unsaturated fats, protein, folic acid, vitamin E and fiber.

Contents per slice

Calories	209
Total fat	6.4 g
saturated fat	0.9 g
monounsaturated fat	3.7 g
polyunsaturated fat	1.8 g
Protein	4.5 g
Carbohydrates	34.2 g
Cholesterol	15.2 mg
Fiber	2.5 g
Calories from fat	28%

Zucchini Lemon Walnut Bread

Fresh bread is one of my greatest weaknesses; it's all I can do to keep myself from slathering warm slices with butter as soon as it comes out of the oven. Fortunately this loaf is moist and delicious enough on its own, and doesn't need butter to help it along. It also keeps really well. To make muffins instead of a loaf, divide the batter among 12 muffin tins that have been sprayed with non-stick spray or lined with paper liners. Bake at 400 F for 20 - 25 minutes, until golden and springy to the touch.

2 cups flour

3/4 cup sugar

1 Tbsp baking powder

1/2 tsp baking soda

1/2 tsp cinnamon (optional)

1/4 tsp salt

1/2 cup milk

1/4 cup canola oil

2 large eggs

grated zest of 1 lemon (optional)

2 cups grated unpeeled zucchini (about 1 large zucchini)

1/2 cup chopped walnuts or pecans

1 Preheat oven to 350 F.

2 In a large bowl, combine the flour, sugar, baking powder, baking soda, cinnamon and salt.

3 In a small bowl, whisk together the milk, oil, eggs and lemon zest and add to the flour mixture along with the grated zucchini and walnuts. Stir by hand just until combined. Don't worry about getting all the lumps out.

4 Pour into an 8" x 4" loaf pan that has been sprayed with non-stick spray and bake for an hour, until golden and springy to the touch. Cool in the pan on a wire rack.

Makes one loaf, about 16 slices.

Contents per slice

Calories	161
Total fat	6.1 g
saturated fat	0.7 g
monounsaturated fat	2.8 g
polyunsaturated fat	2.6 g
Protein	3.7 g
Carbohydrates	22.6 g
Cholesterol	27.2 mg
Fiber	0.8 g
Calories from fat	36%

Cranberry Pumpkin Pecan Bread

I always find myself baking with pumpkin in the fall, when its warmth and aroma seem gratifyingly cozy and old-fashioned. Pumpkin, especially the canned variety, is an excellent source of beta carotene. To make muffins instead of a loaf, divide the batter among 12 muffin tins that have been sprayed with non-stick spray or lined with paper liners. Bake at 400 F for 20 - 25 minutes, until golden and springy to the touch.

1/4 cup butter or stick margarine, softened

1 cup sugar

1 large egg

1 cup canned pure pumpkin

1 tsp vanilla

2 cups flour

1 tsp cinnamon

1 tsp baking powder

1/2 tsp baking soda

1/2 tsp salt

2/3 cup buttermilk

1/2 cup dried cranberries, or 1 cup fresh

1/2 cup chopped pecans

Contents per slice

Calories	170
Total fat	5.4 g
saturated fat	2.2 g
monounsaturated fat	2.4 g
polyunsaturated fat	0.8 g
Protein	2.8 g
Carbohydrates	27.4 g
Cholesterol	21.6 mg
Fiber	1.2 g
Calories from fat	30%

1 Preheat oven to 350 F.

2 In a medium bowl, beat butter and sugar for a minute, until it resembles wet sand. Add egg, pumpkin and vanilla and beat until well blended.

3 In another bowl combine flour, cinnamon, baking powder, baking soda and salt. Add about one third to the butter mixture, beating on low or stirring by hand just until combined. Add half the buttermilk in the same manner, then another one third flour, the remaining buttermilk and remaining flour along with the cranberries and pecans.

4 Pour batter into an 8" x 4" or 9" x 5" loaf pan that has been sprayed with non-stick spray. Bake for one hour and ten minutes, until golden and springy to the touch. Cool in the pan on a wire rack.

Makes one loaf, about 16 slices.

Irish Soda Bread

I'm always amazed that people don't make Irish soda bread more often. It's such an easy way to have freshly baked bread in no time at all! This recipe is perfect if you're too nervous to attempt a yeast bread from scratch – success is all but guaranteed.

2 cups flour

2 cups whole wheat flour

2 Tbsp brown sugar

2 tsp baking powder

1 tsp baking soda

1 tsp salt

1 large egg, slightly beaten

2 cups buttermilk or thin yogurt

flour or old-fashioned rolled oats for kneading

Contents per slice

Calories	132
Total fat	0.7 g
saturated fat	0.3 g
monounsaturated fat	0.2 g
polyunsaturated fat	0.2 g
Protein	5.1 g
Carbohydrates	26.1 g
Cholesterol	14.5 mg
Fiber	2.4 g
Calories from fat	7%

1. Preheat oven to 375 F.

2. In a large bowl, combine all the dry ingredients – flour through salt. In a medium bowl, whisk together the egg and buttermilk, and add all at once to the dry ingredients. Stir until you have a soft ball of dough. While you're mixing, feel free to add any additions you think would be nice – a handful of dried fruit, nuts, grated cheese or fresh herbs.

3. Sprinkle your countertop with a little flour or oats and knead the dough about ten times, forming it into a ball. Place on a baking sheet that has been sprayed with non-stick spray and cut an 'X' lightly on the top.

4. Bake for 45 - 55 minutes, until the loaf is golden and sounds hollow when you tap it on the bottom.

Makes one loaf, about 16 wedges.

Fruit & Nut Soda Bread

Stir 1/2 cup each dried fruit (such as raisins, cranberries or chopped apricots) and chopped nuts (such as walnuts or pecans) into the dough.

Jelly Fauxnuts

Ever since I was a kid I've had a weakness for jelly donuts. These rich and cakey muffins are filled with jam and topped with sugar like jelly doughnuts, but then baked instead of deep fried. This is a great basic muffin recipe to have. Instead of filling them with jelly, you can stir in berries, chopped or dried fruit, grated carrots, zucchini or cheese, nuts, citrus zest – use your imagination! If you don't have buttermilk, use regular milk, a tablespoon of baking powder and no baking soda.

2 cups flour

1/2 cup sugar

2 tsp baking powder

1/2 tsp baking soda

1/2 tsp salt

1 cup buttermilk

3 Tbsp canola oil

1 large egg

2 tsp vanilla

1/4 cup jam, any kind you like

sugar, for sprinkling (optional)

Contents per muffin

Calories	206
Total fat	5.1 g
saturated fat	0.6 g
monounsaturated fat	2.7 g
polyunsaturated fat	1.4 g
Protein	4.1 g
Carbohydrates	35.7 g
Cholesterol	22.4 mg
Fiber	0.9 g
Calories from fat	22%

1. Preheat oven to 400 F.

2. In a large bowl, stir together the flour, sugar, baking powder, baking soda and salt. In a smaller bowl stir together the buttermilk, oil, egg and vanilla. Add to the flour mixture and stir gently just until blended. Don't over mix!

3. Line a muffin pan with paper liners (these tend to stick to paper liners until they are completely cool) or spray with non-stick spray. Put a big spoonful of batter into each cup, make a little dent in the middle and fill with about a teaspoon of jam. Put another spoonful of batter on top, covering the jam completely. Sprinkle with sugar if you like.

4. Bake for about 20 minutes, until golden and springy to the touch. Tip the muffins in their tins to help them cool.

Makes about 10 muffins.

Cheesecake Muffins
Put a small chunk of cream cheese beside the jam in each muffin.

Crumb Cakes
Omit the jam altogether. Stir 1 tsp of cinnamon into 2 Tbsp sugar. Sprinkle the half-filled muffin cups with half the cinnamon sugar, and top with the rest.

Blueberry Lemon Coffee Cake

Simple cakes are always the best, I think. I always use regular or low fat yogurt – never fat-free, which I find gelatinous and unsatisfying. After all, even the 'full fat' varieties usually only have about three grams of fat per serving! This easy-bake cake can be made with fresh or frozen cranberries instead of the blueberries, and orange zest in place of the lemon.

Crumble

1/4 cup flour

1/4 cup packed brown sugar

1 Tbsp butter

1 Tbsp corn syrup or honey

Cake

2 cups flour

1 cup sugar

2 1/2 tsp baking powder

1/2 tsp baking soda

1/2 tsp salt

1 large egg

2 large egg whites

1 cup low-fat or regular yogurt
(plain, vanilla or lemon work best)

1/4 cup butter, melted and cooled

grated zest of 1 lemon or orange (optional)

1 tsp vanilla

2 cups fresh or frozen (unthawed) blueberries

Contents per serving

Calories	190
Total fat	4.0 g
saturated fat	2.5 g
monounsaturated fat	1.2 g
polyunsaturated fat	0.3 g
Protein	3.6 g
Carbohydrates	34.4 g
Cholesterol	24.1 mg
Fiber	1.0 g
Calories from fat	21%

1 Preheat oven to 350 F.

2 To make the crumble topping, combine the flour, brown sugar, butter and corn syrup until well blended and crumbly. Set aside.

3 In a small bowl, toss the berries with about 2 Tbsp flour taken from the 2 cups. In a large bowl combine the remaining flour, sugar, baking powder, baking soda and salt.

4 In a medium bowl, whisk together the egg, egg whites, yogurt, butter, lemon zest and vanilla. Add to the dry ingredients and stir just until blended. Gently fold in the blueberries.

5 Spread the batter into a 9" bundt pan that has been sprayed with non-stick spray, and sprinkle with the crumble mixture. Bake for about an hour and ten minutes, until the cake is springy to the touch. Invert the cake onto a wire rack to cool.

Serves 16.

Caramel Apple Cake

I always hated the expression "have your cake and eat it too" – I mean come on, what good is having a cake if you can't eat it? This recipe makes a pretty big (9" x 13") cake, so it's perfect for sharing. Serve it straight from the pan with coffee or light ice cream. If you don't trust yourself to stop after one piece, wrap individual squares in plastic wrap and freeze them.

2¹/2 cups flour

2 cups sugar

1¹/2 tsp baking soda

¹/2 tsp baking powder

¹/2 tsp salt

1 - 380 mL can evaporated milk

2 large eggs

2 apples, peeled, cored and chopped

¹/3 cup packed brown sugar

¹/2 cup shredded coconut

¹/2 cup chopped pecans

20 unwrapped caramels

Contents per serving

Calories	240
Total fat	3.8 g
saturated fat	1.6 g
monounsaturated fat	1.6 g
polyunsaturated fat	0.6 g
Protein	4.4 g
Carbohydrates	47.5 g
Cholesterol	23.7 mg
Fiber	1.1 g
Calories from fat	15%

1 Preheat oven to 350 F.

2 In a large bowl, combine the flour, sugar, baking soda, baking powder and salt. In a small bowl, stir together 1 cup evaporated milk and the eggs. Add to the dry ingredients along with the apples and stir just until blended.

3 Spread batter into a 9" x 13" pan that has been sprayed with non-stick spray. Sprinkle with brown sugar, coconut and pecans. Bake for 40 - 45 minutes, until golden and springy to the touch. If the top is browning too quickly, cover it loosely with a piece of tin foil.

4 While the cake is baking, combine the remaining evaporated milk and caramels in a small saucepan over medium heat. Cook, stirring occasionally, until melted and smooth. Pour evenly over the cake as soon as it comes out of the oven. Cool completely in the pan on a wire rack.

Serves 20.

Chocolate Cake

What's life without chocolate cake? This is a variation of a recipe I found in an old issue of Eating Well magazine. It's rich, dark and almost chewy, but not too sweet – everything I think a chocolate cake should be. It makes a sturdy bundt cake, which can be served in wedges requiring no more than a napkin and a cold glass of milk. Or it makes three dozen cupcakes – perfect treats for a class or birthday party. The Fluffy White Frosting is light and marshmallowy – it's my favorite – and easily tinted with food coloring for festivities.

2 cups flour

1 cup sugar

3/4 cup cocoa

1¹/2 tsp baking powder

1¹/2 tsp baking soda

1/2 tsp salt

1¹/4 cups buttermilk

1 cup packed brown sugar

3 large egg whites or 2 large eggs

1/4 cup canola oil

2 tsp vanilla

1 cup strong coffee

Fluffy White Frosting (below, optional)

1. Preheat oven to 350 F.

2. In a large bowl, combine flour, sugar, cocoa, baking powder, baking soda and salt.

3. Add buttermilk, brown sugar, egg whites, oil and vanilla and beat for 1 - 2 minutes, until well blended and smooth. Beat in the coffee. The batter will be thin.

4. Pour into a bundt pan that has been sprayed with non-stick spray. Bake for 45 minutes, until the top is springy to the touch.

Serves 16.

Chocolate Zucchini Cake
Stir in 1 zucchini, unpeeled and coarsely grated, along with the coffee. Bake as directed.

Fluffy White Frosting
Dissolve 1¹/2 cups sugar and 1/2 cup water in a saucepan set over low heat. Boil for 7 - 8 minutes, until the mixture reaches 240 F (soft-ball stage) on a candy thermometer. Beat 3 large egg whites in a glass or stainless steel bowl until foamy. Add the sugar syrup in a slow stream and continue beating until the mixture is thick and glossy. Use immediately.

Contents per	slice	cupcake
Calories	208	111
Total fat	3.8 g	2.1 g
saturated fat	0.5 g	0.3 g
monounsaturated fat	2.2 g	1.2 g
polyunsaturated fat	1.1 g	0.6 g
Protein	3.7 g	2.0 g
Carbohydrates	41.3 g	22.0 g
Cholesterol	0.7 mg	0.4 mg
Fiber	2.4 g	1.3 g
Calories from fat	17%	17%

Berry, Peach, Apple or Plum Crumble Cake

This buttery cake wins the Miss Congeniality award by virtue of ease and accessible ingredients. It will enable you to turn a handful of berries or a few humble pieces of fruit into a comforting snack or dessert in 5 minutes. Once you've made it you'll be stirring it up from memory in no time at all. The fruit possibilities are endless. During the summer, peaches and plums are fantastic. During the holidays, scatter a few fresh cranberries over sliced apples or pears and grate a little orange zest into the batter. If you're in a hurry and don't want to bother with the crumble, just sprinkle a little sugar over the fruit before you pop it into the oven.

2 Tbsp butter or margarine, melted

1/2 cup sugar

1 large egg

1 tsp vanilla

1 cup flour

1 tsp baking powder

1/4 tsp salt

1/2 cup milk or plain yogurt

1 - 2 cups fresh or frozen berries

OR 2 peaches, apples or pears

OR 3 - 4 plums, peeled if necessary and sliced

Crumble

1/3 cup flour

1/3 cup packed brown sugar

1/2 tsp cinnamon (optional)

1 Tbsp butter or margarine

2 Tbsp corn syrup or honey

1/4 cup sliced almonds (optional)

Contents per square

Calories	212
Total fat	4.4 g
saturated fat	2.7 g
monounsaturated fat	1.4 g
polyunsaturated fat	0.3 g
Protein	3.2 g
Carbohydrates	39.2 g
Cholesterol	34.8 mg
Fiber	1.4 g
Calories from fat	20%

1 Preheat oven to 400 F.

2 In a medium bowl, beat the butter and sugar until well blended. Beat in egg and vanilla.

3 In a small bowl, combine the flour, baking powder and salt. Add half to the butter mixture and beat just until blended. Add the milk and beat just until combined. Add the remaining flour mixture and beat on low until just combined.

4 Spread the batter into an 8" x 8" pan that has been sprayed with non-stick spray. Sprinkle with berries or layer the sliced fruit over top, placing the slices close together or overlapping them – fruit shrinks as it cooks. In a small bowl stir together the flour, brown sugar, cinnamon, butter and corn syrup with a fork or your fingers until it's well combined. Stir in almonds and sprinkle over the fruit.

5 Bake for 30 - 40 minutes, until golden and springy to the touch. Cool in the pan.

Makes 9 squares.

Blackberry Upside-Down Cake
Scatter 2 cups fresh blackberries over the bottom of a parchment-lined pan. Sprinkle with 2 Tbsp sugar. Pour cake batter over top and bake as directed; omit the crumble. Invert onto a plate while still warm.

Date Squares

Known in the old days as Matrimonial Slice, this is one of few recipes to survive generations virtually unscathed. Comfort takes precedence over glamour, making these popular at trendy eateries everywhere. This version contains less than half the fat of a traditional recipe.

Base & Topping

1 cup flour

1 cup oats

2/3 cup packed brown sugar

1/4 tsp baking soda

1/4 tsp salt

1/3 cup butter, melted

1 Tbsp corn syrup or honey

Filling

1/2 lb (250 g) pitted dates, chopped (about 2 cups)

1/3 cup packed brown sugar

1 cup water or orange juice

1 Tbsp lemon juice

Contents per square

Calories	196
Total fat	4.2 g
saturated fat	2.5 g
monounsaturated fat	1.3 g
polyunsaturated fat	0.4 g
Protein	2.8 g
Carbohydrates	37.7 g
Cholesterol	10.4 mg
Fiber	1.6 g
Calories from fat	21%

1 Preheat oven to 350 F.

2 In a large bowl, combine flour, oats, brown sugar, baking soda and salt. Add butter and corn syrup and blend until the mixture is well combined and crumbly. Press half the crumbs into an 8" x 8" pan that has been sprayed with non-stick spray.

3 Combine dates, brown sugar and water in a small saucepan over medium heat. Bring to a simmer and cook, stirring often, for 5 - 10 minutes or until thick. Remove from heat and stir in lemon juice.

4 Spread the filling over the base and sprinkle with the remaining crumb mixture, squeezing it as you go to make bigger clumps. Bake for 30 minutes, until golden around the edges. Cool in the pan on a wire rack.

Makes 16 squares.

Berry Oat Squares

Stir together 2 cups fresh or frozen berries, 1/2 cup berry jam and 2 tsp flour; use in place of the date filling.

One Bite Brownies

Have you ever had those One Bite Brownies you can buy in little brown paper bags at the grocery store? They're awesome, mostly because they're loaded with fat. These only have 2 grams per pop, and will definitely satisfy your need for brownies. Be careful not to overbake them – they should be slightly puffed but still soft to the touch. If you don't have mini muffin cups, the batter can be baked in an 8" x 8" pan at 350 F for 25 - 30 minutes. Freeze leftovers and serve them with light ice cream and chocolate syrup!

1/4 cup butter or stick margarine, softened

1 1/4 cups sugar

1 large egg

2 large egg whites

1 tsp vanilla

1 tsp instant coffee granules, dissolved in 1 tsp water

1 cup flour

1/2 cup cocoa

1/4 tsp baking powder

1/4 tsp salt

1. Preheat oven to 350 F.

2. In a large bowl, mix together butter and sugar until well combined. Add egg, egg whites, vanilla and coffee and stir until well blended and smooth.

3. In a medium bowl, combine flour, cocoa, baking powder and salt. Add to the egg mixture and stir by hand just until combined.

4. Spoon the batter into mini muffin cups that have been sprayed with non-stick spray. Bake for 12 - 15 minutes, until puffed but still soft to the touch. Do not overbake! Cool in the pan on a wire rack.

Makes 24 - 30 brownies.

Contents per brownie

Calories	85
Total fat	2.1 g
saturated fat	1.3 g
monounsaturated fat	0.7 g
polyunsaturated fat	0.1 g
Protein	1.5 g
Carbohydrates	15.5 g
Cholesterol	14.2 mg
Fiber	1.0 g
Calories from fat	23%

Salad Bars

Necessity is the mother of invention, as evidenced every August when I end up with armloads of zucchini. In an attempt to use up my stash, I thought I'd make a carrot–zucchini cake, and added a dollop of tomato paste (ever hear of Tomato Soup Cake?) to add moisture and a vitamin boost. The result was a deliciously moist low-fat cake that's perfect topped with lemony cream cheese frosting. No one will ever guess these cakey bars have three veggies in them!

3 Tbsp butter or margarine, softened

3/4 cup packed brown sugar

1 large egg

1 tsp vanilla

1 cup flour

1 tsp baking soda

1/4 - 1/2 tsp cinnamon

1/4 tsp salt

pinch allspice

1 small zucchini, unpeeled and grated

1 carrot, peeled and grated

1 Tbsp tomato paste

1/2 cup raisins or dried cranberries

1/4 cup chopped pecans or walnuts

Cream Cheese Frosting

1/4 cup light cream cheese, softened

1 Tbsp lemon juice or water

1 1/2 cups icing sugar

Contents per bar

Calories	233
Total fat	5.4 g
saturated fat	2.6 g
monounsaturated fat	2.2 g
polyunsaturated fat	0.6 g
Protein	2.7 g
Carbohydrates	43.8 g
Cholesterol	28.8 mg
Fiber	1.4 g
Calories from fat	22%

1 Preheat oven to 350 F.

2 In a large bowl, beat the butter, brown sugar, egg and vanilla until smooth. In a small bowl, combine the flour, baking soda, cinnamon, salt and allspice.

3 Add the flour mixture to the egg mixture along with the grated zucchini, carrot, tomato paste, raisins and walnuts, and stir by hand just until combined. Spread the batter in an 8" x 8" pan that has been sprayed with non-stick spray.

4 Bake for 25 - 30 minutes, until golden and springy to the touch. Cool in the pan on a wire rack.

5 To make the cream cheese frosting, beat the cream cheese until fluffy. Add the lemon juice and icing sugar and beat until smooth. Add a little extra sugar or lemon juice if you need to achieve a spreadable consistency. Frost when the squares are cool.

Makes 12 bars.

Clockwise from bottom left:
Roasted Pearl Onion Crostini
Curried Peanut Shrimp
Balsamic Mushroom Crostini

Clockwise from bottom left:
Jalapeno Poppers
Calzone
Stromboli
Potato Skins

Top to bottom:
Sesame Snaps
Mini Toad in the Hole
Tuna Stuffed Tomatoes

Top to bottom:
Sticky, Spicy Drumsticks
Chicken, Black Bean & Mushroom Quesadillas
Stuffed Pizza Bites

Peanut Butter Power Bars

I developed this recipe after buying an amazing power bar at a trendy coffee shop – and figured at $3 each I should probably attempt to make them myself. These are perfect for those days when you need a little ammo in your bag to combat the vending machine. They can be made with any combination of dried fruit, nuts and seeds that you like, but the more the merrier! A pinch of cinnamon is good too.

1/2 cup packed brown sugar

1/4 cup light peanut butter

1/4 cup soy or regular milk

1/4 cup honey or molasses

2 Tbsp canola oil

1 tsp vanilla

3/4 cup whole wheat flour

3/4 cup oats

1/2 tsp baking soda

pinch salt

1/2 cup raisins and/or dried cranberries

1/2 cup chocolate chips

1/4 cup sliced almonds

1/4 cup sunflower seeds and/or pumpkin seeds

1/4 cup shredded coconut (optional)

2 Tbsp ground flax seed

1 Preheat oven to 350 F.

2 In a large bowl, stir together the brown sugar, peanut butter, milk, honey, oil and vanilla. In a small bowl, stir together the flour, oats, baking soda and salt.

3 Add the oat mixture to the peanut butter mixture along with the raisins, chocolate chips, almonds, sunflower seeds, coconut and flaxseed; stir until well blended.

4 Spread the batter into a 9" x 13" pan that has been sprayed with non-stick spray. The mixture will be sticky – I usually use my hands, dampening them first. Bake for 20 - 25 minutes, until golden. Cool in the pan on a wire rack.

Makes 18 bars.

Contents per bar

Calories	161
Total fat	6.1 g
saturated fat	1.4 g
monounsaturated fat	2.8 g
polyunsaturated fat	1.9 g
Protein	3.1 g
Carbohydrates	25.4 g
Cholesterol	0.0 mg
Fiber	2.1 g
Calories from fat	34%

Savory Pistachio and Olive Biscotti

The idea for this unique flavor combination comes from Martha Stewart, who I think has great taste. Savory biscotti go really well with wine and cheese or a plate of crackers when you're serving dip.

2¹/2 cups flour

2 tsp baking powder

¹/4 tsp each salt & pepper

grated zest of one lemon

¹/4 cup butter

1 large egg

2 large egg whites

¹/2 cup milk

¹/2 cup shelled pistachios, salted or unsalted

¹/2 cup black olives, pitted and finely chopped

Contents per biscotti

Calories	91
Total fat	3.8 g
saturated fat	1.5 g
monounsaturated fat	1.9 g
polyunsaturated fat	0.4 g
Protein	2.5 g
Carbohydrates	11.1 g
Cholesterol	14.4 mg
Fiber	0.7 g
Calories from fat	40%

1. Preheat oven to 350 F.

2. In the bowl of a food processor combine flour, baking powder, salt, pepper and lemon zest and pulse to blend.

3. In a small saucepan, melt the butter over medium heat. Continue to cook, swirling the pan often, for 5 - 7 minutes or until it turns deep brown. Set aside to cool slightly.

4. Pour the browned butter slowly through the feed tube of the food processor with the machine running, and process until the mixture resembles wet sand. Transfer to a large mixing bowl.

5. In a small bowl, whisk together the egg, egg whites and milk. Add to the flour mixture and stir until the dough begins to come together. Add the pistachios and olives and mix until the dough is combined (you may have to use your hands).

6. On a lightly-floured surface, divide the dough in half and shape each piece into an 8" log. Place the logs 2" - 3" apart on a cookie sheet that has been sprayed with non-stick spray, and flatten each so that it is about 3" wide. If you like, brush the tops with some beaten egg white to give them a shiny finish.

**Savory Pistachio
and Olive Biscotti continued**

The World's Best Peanut Butter Cookies

Everybody says these are the best peanut butter cookies they've ever eaten. Because they contain no flour, they're great for people with gluten intolerance.

7 Bake the logs for 25 - 30 minutes, until firm and starting to crack on top. Cool the logs on a wire rack and reduce oven temperature to 275 F.

8 Place the logs on a cutting board and slice 1/2" thick with a sharp, serrated knife. Place the biscotti upright on the cookie sheet and bake for another 20 minutes, until slightly golden. Cool on the pan or transfer to a wire rack.

Makes about 2 dozen biscotti.

Sun-dried Tomato & Parmesan Biscotti
Substitute 1/2 cup grated Parmesan cheese, a small handful of chopped sun-dried tomatoes and a few capers for the pistachios and olives.

1¹/2 cups light peanut butter

1/2 cup sugar

¹/2 cup packed brown sugar

1 large egg white

1 Preheat oven to 350 F.

2 In a large bowl, stir together the peanut butter, sugar, brown sugar and egg white until completely blended.

3 Roll dough into 1¹/2" balls and place about 2" apart on an ungreased cookie sheet. Press down on each cookie once or twice with the back of a fork.

4 Bake for 12 - 15 minutes, until very pale golden around the edges. Gently transfer to a wire rack to cool.

Makes 2 dozen cookies.

Contents per cookie

Calories	110
Total fat	5.3 g
saturated fat	1.0 g
monounsaturated fat	2.4 g
polyunsaturated fat	1.9 g
Protein	14.1 g
Carbohydrates	0.0 g
Cholesterol	57.5 mg
Fiber	0.8 g
Calories from fat	41%

Breakfast Bean Cookies

It's amazing what passes as breakfast these days – rainbow-colored Pop Tarts, Krispy Kremes and chocolate cereal. Even the once virtuous muffin often resembles a giant cupcake. I developed this recipe for my eleven-year-old friend Kyla, when she was in the hospital and didn't have much of an appetite. I wondered how to sneak as much nutrition as possible into a cookie, and the answer was obvious – beans are packed with protein, fiber, vitamins and minerals. Pureed, you don't even know they're there! These substantial, not-too-sweet cookies have an amazingly tender texture, keep longer than other low fat cookies, and make a great breakfast in the car.

2 cups oats

1 cup flour

1 tsp baking powder

1 tsp baking soda

1/4 tsp cinnamon

1/4 tsp salt

1 - 14 oz (398 mL) can white kidney, navy or cannellini beans, rinsed and drained

1/4 cup butter or margarine, softened

1 cup packed brown sugar

1 large egg

1 tsp vanilla

1/2 cup chocolate chips (optional)

1/2 cup raisins or dried cranberries

1/4 - 1/2 cup chopped walnuts or pecans

2 Tbsp ground flaxseed (optional)

Contents per cookie

Calories	138
Total fat	3.2 g
saturated fat	1.4 g
monounsaturated fat	1.0 g
polyunsaturated fat	0.8 g
Protein	3.4 g
Carbohydrates	23.9 g
Cholesterol	14.2 mg
Fiber	2.0 g
Calories from fat	22%

1 Preheat oven to 350 F.

2 Place oats in the bowl of a food processor and pulse until it resembles coarse flour. Add the flour, baking powder, baking soda, cinnamon and salt and whiz until combined. Transfer to a large bowl.

3 Put the beans into the food processor and pulse until smooth, scraping down the sides of the bowl. Add butter and process until well blended. Add the brown sugar, egg and vanilla and pulse until smooth, scraping down the sides of the bowl.

4 Pour the bean mixture into the oat mixture and stir by hand until almost combined; add the chocolate chips, raisins, nuts and flaxseed and stir just until blended.

5 Drop large spoonfuls of dough onto a cookie sheet that has been sprayed with non-stick spray, and flatten each one a little with your hand. (I find this works best if I dampen my hands first.) Bake for 14 - 16 minutes, until pale golden around the edges but still soft in the middle. Transfer to a wire rack to cool.

Makes 2 dozen cookies.

Cranberry, Orange & White Chocolate Chunk Cookies

I have a recipe in my first book, *One Smart Cookie*, for chewy cranberry orange cookies. One Christmas my friend Joni baked me a batch of cookies with white chocolate chunks in them and I thought they were the best cookies I had ever tasted. She said thanks – they're from your book! Now I only make them with white chocolate. People go mad for them any time of the year.

1/4 cup butter or stick margarine, softened

1/2 cup sugar

1/2 cup packed brown sugar

grated zest of 1 orange

1 large egg

3 Tbsp orange juice

1 tsp vanilla

1 1/2 cups flour

1/2 tsp baking powder

1/2 tsp baking soda

1/4 tsp salt

1 cup fresh or frozen (unthawed) cranberries, coarsely chopped

1/2 cup white chocolate chunks or chips

1 Preheat oven to 350 F.

2 In a large bowl, beat the butter, sugar, brown sugar and orange zest until well blended – the mixture will look like wet sand. Add the egg, orange juice, and vanilla and beat until smooth.

3 In a small bowl, combine the flour, baking powder, baking soda and salt. Add to the sugar mixture and stir by hand until almost combined; add the cranberries and white chocolate and stir just until blended.

4 Drop spoonfuls of dough about 1" apart on a cookie sheet that has been sprayed with non-stick spray. Bake for 12 - 15 minutes, until barely golden and set around the edges but still soft in the middle. Transfer to a wire rack to cool.

Makes 1 1/2 dozen cookies.

Contents per cookie

Calories	135
Total fat	4.0 g
saturated fat	2.5 g
monounsaturated fat	1.3 g
polyunsaturated fat	2.0 g
Protein	1.7 g
Carbohydrates	23.3 g
Cholesterol	18.9 mg
Fiber	0.9 g
Calories from fat	28%

Ginger Molasses Crinkles

Every time I make these, everyone claims they are their absolute favorite kind of cookie. A stack of them looks great wrapped in cellophane and tied with a ribbon. If you don't have fresh ginger, add 1/2 tsp ground ginger along with the cinnamon. These are worth baking just for the smell of it!

2 Tbsp canola oil

2 Tbsp butter or margarine, softened

1/3 cup dark molasses

1 cup packed brown sugar

1 Tbsp grated fresh ginger

2 large egg whites or 1 large egg

1 tsp vanilla

1 cup flour

1 cup whole wheat flour

2 tsp baking soda

2 tsp cinnamon

1/2 tsp salt

sugar for rolling

Contents per cookie

Calories	107
Total fat	2.1 g
saturated fat	0.7 g
monounsaturated fat	1.0 g
polyunsaturated fat	0.4 g
Protein	1.5 g
Carbohydrates	20.7 g
Cholesterol	2.6 mg
Fiber	0.8 g
Calories from fat	18%

1. Preheat oven to 350 F.

2. In a large bowl, combine the oil, butter, molasses, brown sugar, ginger, egg whites and vanilla. Stir until well blended.

3. In a medium bowl, combine flours, baking soda, cinnamon and salt; add to the molasses mixture and stir by hand just until you have a soft dough. Don't over mix!

4. Roll the dough into 1" - 1 1/2" balls and roll the balls in sugar to coat. Place 1" apart on a cookie sheet that has been sprayed with non-stick spray.

5. Bake for 12 - 14 minutes, until just set around the edges. Transfer to a wire rack to cool. Store extras in an airtight container or freeze.

Makes 2 dozen cookies.

Ginger Molasses Crinkle Sandwiches
Spread the underside of half the cooled cookies with the Cream Cheese Frosting on page 156, and sandwich with another cookie.

Chocolate Mint Meringues

There aren't many things in the world that are both fat-free and melt-in-your-mouth. The combination of egg whites and sugar – the basis for all meringues – is just that. Meringues are baked for a long time at a low temperature to make them crisp, and then cooled in the oven to dry them out – they shouldn't be sticky. If you want to bake the whole batch at once, spread the meringue in a thin layer over a prepared cookie sheet and bake as directed, then break into pieces like bark.

4 large egg whites

1/4 tsp cream of tartar

1/2 cup sugar

3/4 cup icing sugar

3 peppermint candy canes

1/2 cup chocolate chips, coarsely chopped

Contents per meringue

Calories	39
Total fat	0.6 g
saturated fat	0.4 g
monounsaturated fat	0.2 g
polyunsaturated fat	0.0 g
Protein	0.5 g
Carbohydrates	8.3 g
Cholesterol	0.0 mg
Fiber	0.1 g
Calories from fat	15%

1 Preheat oven to 225 F.

2 Line two baking sheets with parchment paper. Place candy canes in a zip-lock baggie and bash with a rolling pin until they are coarsely crushed.

3 Place egg whites and cream of tartar in a glass or stainless steel bowl and beat at medium speed until soft peaks form. Increase speed to high and gradually add sugars, beating until stiff peaks form. Fold in crushed candy and chocolate.

4 Drop the meringue mixture in spoonfuls onto the prepared sheets, swirling the tops. Bake for 1 1/2 hours; turn the oven off and let them cool in the closed oven for 2 hours. Carefully peel the meringues from the paper.

Makes about 3 dozen meringues.

Chocolate Apricot Pecan Meringues
Replace the candy canes with 1/4 cup each coarsely-chopped dried apricots and toasted pecans or hazelnuts.

Coconut Meringues
Replace the candy canes and chocolate with 1/2 tsp coconut extract and 1 cup toasted shredded coconut.

Peppermint Patties

I've always loved those chocolate mint Girl Guide cookies, and I'm not the only one – apparently they are the #1 best-selling cookies in North America! Here's a homemade version. To fancy these up, dip each cookie in melted chocolate or roll the edges in crushed candy canes for a crunchy and decorative edge. Or best of all, instead of filling them with icing, place an After Eight mint between 2 cookies as soon as they come out of the oven and press a little to make the chocolate melt (adds about 1 gram of fat per cookie).

Chocolate Cookies

1/4 cup butter, softened

1/2 cup sugar

1/2 cup packed brown sugar

1 large egg white

1 tsp instant coffee, dissolved in 1 Tbsp water

1 tsp vanilla

1 cup flour

1/2 cup cocoa

1/4 tsp baking soda

1/4 tsp salt

Filling

1 1/2 cups icing sugar

1 1/2 Tbsp water

1/2 tsp peppermint extract

Contents per sandwich

Calories	124
Total fat	2.3 g
saturated fat	1.5 g
monounsaturated fat	0.7 g
polyunsaturated fat	0.1 g
Protein	1.3 g
Carbohydrates	25.4 g
Cholesterol	6.2 mg
Fiber	1.2 g
Calories from fat	17%

1 In a large bowl, beat together butter and sugars until well combined – the mixture will have the consistency of wet sand. Beat in egg white, coffee and vanilla until smooth.

2 In a medium bowl combine flour, cocoa, baking soda and salt. Add to the egg mixture and stir by hand just until blended. Shape the dough into a disk, wrap in plastic and refrigerate for an hour or until chilled.

3 Preheat oven to 350 F.

4 Roll dough out 1/8" thick between two sheets of waxed paper or on a lightly floured surface. Cut into 2" - 2 1/2" rounds with a cookie cutter or into squares with a knife. Reroll the scraps once to get as many cookies as you can. Place about an inch apart on an ungreased cookie sheet and bake for 10 - 12 minutes, until set. Transfer to a wire rack to cool.

5 Stir together the icing sugar, water and peppermint extract to make the filling. Spread half of the cooled cookies with the frosting and top with a second cookie.

Makes about 20 sandwiches.

Rye Raisin Crackers

Although I felt compelled to call these crackers, they aren't the kind that are conducive to scooping up dips. They are the kind you eat all by themselves or with a slice of cheddar cheese. I absolutely adore these. They are halfway between a cracker and a cookie, but not too sweet (usually not a selling point for me) and very plain. I love the crunchiness of the crackers with the chewiness of the raisins.

1^1/2 cups flour

1 cup rye or whole wheat flour

2 Tbsp brown sugar

1 tsp baking powder

^{1}/2 tsp salt

^{1}/4 cup butter or stick margarine

^{1}/2 cup water

1 cup raisins

Contents per cracker

Calories	50
Total fat	1.1 g
saturated fat	0.7 g
monounsaturated fat	0.3 g
polyunsaturated fat	0.1 g
Protein	1.0 g
Carbohydrates	9.3 g
Cholesterol	3.0 mg
Fiber	0.8 g
Calories from fat	21%

1. Preheat oven to 350 F.

2. In the bowl of a food processor, combine flours, brown sugar, baking powder and salt. Add the butter and pulse until the mixture is well blended.

3. Transfer to a large bowl and add the water. Stir just until the dough comes together. Knead the dough gently a few times and then divide it in half.

4. Roll each piece out on a clean surface until they're about ^{1}/8" thick and roughly the same size. Sprinkle one piece of dough evenly with raisins, lay the other piece on top and roll it again to squish them together. Gently roll until it becomes one piece again, and you can pick it up and flip it over. Continue rolling until you have a large rectangle that is ^{1}/4" thick or thinner, and the raisins almost come through the surface. Cut into squares or rectangles with a pizza wheel or knife and transfer to an ungreased cookie sheet.

5. Bake for 15 - 20 minutes, until pale golden around the edges. Transfer to a wire rack to cool.

Makes 3^1/2 dozen 1^1/2" x 2" crackers.

Biscuits

Buttermilk makes these biscuits very tender, and the soda is added to neutralize its acidity. If you want to use regular milk instead, omit the baking soda. Biscuits are always best when they're fresh, but they are so quick to make you don't really need to make them in advance. To make sweet biscuits to split and fill with berries and thick vanilla yogurt, add a tablespoon of sugar to the flour mixture.

2 cups flour

1 Tbsp baking powder

¹/₄ tsp baking soda

¹/₂ tsp salt

¹/₄ cup butter or canola oil

1 cup buttermilk

1 Preheat the oven to 450 F.

2 In a large bowl, combine the flour, baking powder, baking soda and salt. Cut in the butter or pour in the oil and blend until the mixture resembles coarse meal. Add the buttermilk and stir just until the dough forms a ball.

3 On a lightly floured surface, gently knead the dough four or five times. Pat the dough about ¹/₂" thick and cut into circles with a biscuit cutter, glass rim or the open end of a tin can.

4 Place the biscuits on an ungreased baking sheet. If you like, brush the tops with a little milk.

5 Bake for 13 - 15 minutes, until golden. Serve right away, while they're still warm.

Makes about a dozen 2" biscuits.

Cheese Biscuits

Stir 1 cup grated old cheddar cheese (or any kind of cheese you like) into the flour mixture after you have cut in the butter. Mix and bake as directed.

Parmesan, Olive & Sun-dried Tomato Biscuits

Stir a few chopped black olives, a few chopped sun-dried tomatoes and 2 Tbsp grated parmesan cheese into the flour mixture after you blend in the butter. Mix and bake as directed. These are great cut into tiny (1") rounds, split and spread with a mild, soft cheese for a party.

Chocolate Biscuits

Stir ¹/₂ cup cocoa into the flour mixture before you cut in the butter. These are great with berries and good vanilla yogurt!

Contents per biscuit

Calories	119
Total fat	3.9 g
saturated fat	2.5 g
monounsaturated fat	1.2 g
polyunsaturated fat	0.2 g
Protein	2.9 g
Carbohydrates	17.1 g
Cholesterol	11.0 mg
Fiber	0.6 g
Calories from fat	32%

Cinnamon Sticky Biscuits

I have to say this is one of my favorite recipes of all time. I am such a sucker for cinnamon sticky buns, but at about 700 calories and 30-plus grams of fat in many bakery cinnamon buns, I can't afford to indulge very often! These are great because the biscuit dough doesn't require any rising, which is important when you need to satisfy a craving NOW. My Mom used to make cinnamon biscuits for dessert when there wasn't anything else around. Try laying thin slices of these biscuits on top of a dish of peaches or apples tossed with sugar, then bake at 350 F. for 20-30 minutes for a phenomenal fruit cobbler.

Stickiness

2 Tbsp butter

1/4 cup packed brown sugar

1 Tbsp honey or corn syrup

Biscuits

2 cups flour

1 Tbsp baking powder

1 Tbsp sugar

1/4 tsp salt

3/4 cup milk

1/4 cup canola oil

Filling

1/2 cup packed brown sugar

1/2 tsp cinnamon

1/4 cup raisins and/or chopped pecans (optional)

Contents per biscuit

Calories	270
Total fat	8.6 g
saturated fat	2.2 g
monounsaturated fat	4.4 g
polyunsaturated fat	2.0 g
Protein	3.6 g
Carbohydrates	44.0 g
Cholesterol	7.7 mg
Fiber	0.9 g
Calories from fat	30%

1. Preheat oven to 400 F.

2. Combine butter, brown sugar and honey in a small saucepan or microwave-safe bowl and heat until melted and smooth. Pour over the bottom of an 8" x 8" baking pan that has been sprayed with non-stick spray.

3. In a large bowl, combine flour, baking powder, sugar and salt. Add the milk and canola oil and stir by hand just until you have a soft dough. Do not over mix!

4. On a lightly floured surface, pat or roll the dough into a 9" x 14" rectangle. Sprinkle with brown sugar, cinnamon and raisins or nuts. Starting from a long side, roll tightly jelly-roll style into a log. Cut into nine biscuits using dental floss or a serrated knife, and place cut side down in the pan.

5. Bake for 20 minutes, until golden and bubbly. Invert onto a platter while still warm.

Makes 9 sticky biscuits.

Garlic Cheese Rolls
Omit stickiness and filling. Spread the rolled dough with a mixture of 1 Tbsp butter or oil and 2 crushed cloves of garlic. Sprinkle with 1/2 cup grated old cheddar cheese; roll and bake as directed.

Bagels

Bagels are easy to buy, but almost as easy to make yourself. If you're like me and love to bake, you may even find the process therapeutic! And nothing beats a hot bagel straight from the oven. The problem with store-bought bagels is their size – the ones that are close to the size of your head can weigh in at 500 calories apiece, even though they are low in fat. You can flavor these any way you like by stirring in some grated cheese, caramelized onions, fresh garlic, dried blueberries, toasted nuts or seeds.

3^1/4 tsp active dry yeast

1 Tbsp brown sugar

1 Tbsp canola oil

4 - 5 cups all-purpose flour

2 tsp salt

sesame, poppy or caraway seed to sprinkle on top (optional)

Contents per bagel

Calories	222
Total fat	1.7 g
saturated fat	0.2 g
monounsaturated fat	0.9 g
polyunsaturated fat	0.6 g
Protein	5.8 g
Carbohydrates	44.3 g
Cholesterol	0.0 mg
Fiber	1.7 g
Calories from fat	8%

1. In a large bowl, stir yeast and brown sugar into 1^1/2 cups lukewarm water until it dissolves; let it stand for five minutes until it gets foamy. If it doesn't, the yeast is probably expired – toss it and get some fresh yeast!

2. Stir the oil and 1 cup flour into the yeast mixture, then add the salt and enough of the remaining flour to make a soft dough – I usually use about 2^1/2 cups. Turn the dough out onto a lightly floured surface and knead, gently incorporating more flour, until the dough is smooth and elastic. It should take about ten minutes. Cover with a tea towel and let it rest for about 15 minutes.

3. Divide the dough into ten pieces. Roll each piece into a rope and then shape it into a circle, pinching the ends together to form bagels. Let them rise for about 20 minutes while you boil a big pot (about 6L) of salted water and preheat the oven to 450 F.

4. When the water comes to a boil, reduce the heat to a simmer and gently place a few bagels at a time into the water. Simmer for one minute, then flip them over and cook for another 30 seconds. Remove them with a slotted spoon and place on a wire

Onion Bialys

Named for the Polish city of Bialystok, a bialy is a chewy, round yeast roll similar to a bagel. It has a depression rather than a hole in the center, and is sprinkled with chopped onion before baking.

rack to drain. Once they have all been boiled, place them on a cookie sheet that has been sprayed with non-stick spray, and sprinkle with sesame seeds or whatever toppings you like.

5 Place in the oven, reduce heat to 425 F and bake for 20 minutes, until golden.

Makes 10 bagels.

Cinnamon Raisin Bagels

Add 1 tsp cinnamon and 1/2 - 1 cup raisins along with the second batch of flour. Mix and bake as directed.

Onion & Garlic Bagels

Sauté 1 minced onion and a few cloves of crushed garlic in 1 tsp oil until tender and golden. Cool and stir into the dough along with the second batch of flour. Mix and bake as directed.

Cheese Bagels

Add 1 tsp garlic powder and 1 cup grated old cheddar or 1/2 cup grated Parmesan cheese along with the second batch of flour. Sprinkle the tops with a little extra grated cheese if you like.

1 batch bagel dough (previous page)
1 large onion, finely chopped
1 Tbsp poppy seed
1 Tbsp canola oil
cornmeal, for sprinkling on baking sheet
1 egg (optional)
salt, for sprinkling

1 Once the dough has risen, punch it down and shape into 12 pieces. Cover with a towel and let rest for 10 minutes, then shape each into a 4" - 5" oval, like a small pizza. Place on a baking sheet that has been sprinkled with cornmeal.

2 If you want a shiny finish, brush the bialys with beaten egg. Stir together the onion, poppy seed and canola oil and place a spoonful on top of each bialy. Sprinkle with salt. Cover with a tea towel and let rise for another half an hour; preheat oven to 425 F.

3 Bake the bialys for 20 - 25 minutes, until golden.

Makes 12 bialys.

Focaccia

Focaccia dough is a lot like pizza dough, but the result is more like a thick flatbread with less stuff on top. Tear it up to use as a dipper or split and fill it to make a sandwich. Focaccia stuffed with tuna and roasted red peppers or roasted vegetables and cheese is fantastic! When you pat out the dough, you can make a single loaf or cut it with a small biscuit cutter into mini focaccias. These go very well with any kind of spread or can be used in place of crostini.

3/4 cup warm water

1/2 tsp sugar

1 1/2 tsp active dry yeast

2 1/4 - 2 1/2 cups flour

1 tsp salt

grinding of fresh black pepper

1 Tbsp olive oil

Topping

1 Tbsp olive oil

2 cloves garlic, crushed, or 1 Tbsp chopped fresh rosemary or thyme

1 tsp coarse salt

Contents per wedge

Calories	216
Total fat	4.7 g
saturated fat	0.7 g
monounsaturated fat	3.4 g
polyunsaturated fat	0.6 g
Protein	5.3 g
Carbohydrates	36.8 g
Cholesterol	0.0 mg
Fiber	1.7 g
Calories from fat	21%

1. Combine water and sugar in a large bowl; sprinkle with yeast and let stand until foamy. If the yeast doesn't foam, it is either inactive or the water you used was too hot and killed it. Buy fresh yeast or try again!

2. Stir in 2 cups flour, salt, pepper and olive oil. Knead in enough of the remaining flour until you have a soft dough. Knead for a few minutes, until it's smooth and elastic.

3. Transfer the dough to an oiled bowl (roll the dough in the bowl so it gets coated with oil too), cover with a tea towel and let it rise in a warm place until doubled in bulk – about 45 minutes. If you want to make this ahead, let it rise slowly in the fridge covered with plastic wrap for 24 hours.

4. Pat the dough into a 9" - 10" circle on a baking sheet. Poke holes with your finger all over the top and drizzle with oil, garlic and salt. Cover loosely with plastic wrap and let rise for about an hour, until doubled. Preheat the oven to 400 F.

5. Bake focaccia for 20 - 30 minutes, until it's golden and sounds hollow when tapped.

Makes one focaccia; serves about 6.

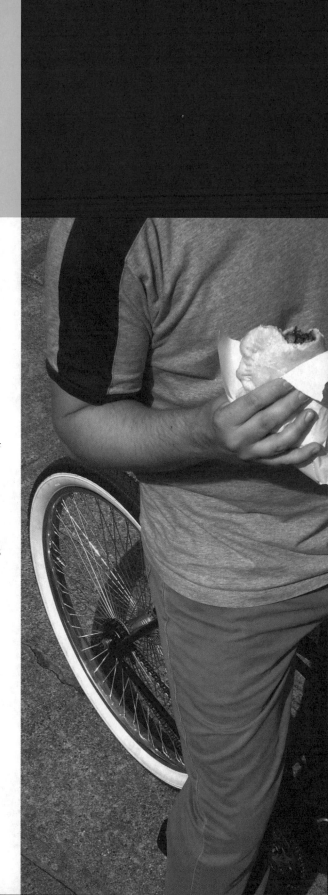

Caramelized Onion & Parmesan Focaccia
Toss a thinly sliced onion with 1 Tbsp olive or canola oil and spread over the unbaked dough. Sprinkle with 1 Tbsp grated Parmesan cheese and bake as directed, adding a few extra minutes to the baking time.

Olive & Feta Focaccia
Add $1/4$ cup chopped Kalamata olives to the dough along with the olive oil. Shape and poke the dough as directed, then top with $1/4$ cup crumbled feta and a drizzle of olive oil before baking.

Grape Focaccia
Instead of drizzling the poked dough with olive oil, scatter with about a cup of small or halved seedless purple grapes and press them into the dough. Sprinkle with some chopped walnuts or fresh rosemary and $1/4$ cup sugar – coarse sugar is perfect if you can get it – and bake as directed. Or omit the sugar and sprinkle the baked focaccia with icing sugar.

Sweet Eats

Everyone needs a little something sweet sometimes. Fudge is good for the soul. Peanut brittle always makes me happy. We eat for many reasons that have nothing to do with nutrition, and that's OK – so long as Ben & Jerry haven't become your closest friends.

All of the sweets in this chapter will satisfy a sweet tooth with less fat than traditional desserts. If you're a chocoholic, don't think you have to go without... chocolate contains the same antioxidants as red wine and green tea, and the darker the better. If you're a purist, chocolate that contains over 60% cocoa is the best choice. When you need some, indulge in a small piece of the very best chocolate you can find – there's no substitute for the real thing!

Stone Fruit Tarts

Day-old bread absorbs the juices and sugar to make a wonderfully chewy, low-fat crust for these 'tarts', which make a great breakfast! Double or triple the recipe according to how many people you want to feed. You can even make them for one in your toaster oven. This will become one of those things you make all the time without even needing the recipe.

8 - 1/2" thick slices day old plain or sourdough baguette

1 Tbsp butter, softened

2 - 4 peaches, nectarines and/or plums

1/4 cup packed brown sugar

pinch cinnamon, optional

Contents per tart

Calories	120
Total fat	2.0 g
saturated fat	1.1 g
monounsaturated fat	0.7 g
polyunsaturated fat	0.2 g
Protein	2.5 g
Carbohydrates	22.7 g
Cholesterol	3.9 mg
Fiber	1.1 g
Calories from fat	16%

1. Preheat oven to 350 F.

2. Lightly butter each slice of bread and place butter-side-up on a cookie sheet. Peel the nectarines and plums if you like (I leave the skins on), and slice them thickly. Put some brown sugar in a shallow dish and roll the slices of fruit in the sugar to coat well.

3. Arrange a few wedges of fruit closely on each slice of bread, and sprinkle with any leftover sugar. If you like, sprinkle them with cinnamon. Bake for 12 - 15 minutes, until the fruit is soft. Serve warm, but allow them to cool for a bit first – the fruit gets very hot!

Serves 4.

Puffed Wheat Squares

The great thing about recipes like puffed wheat and Rice Krispie squares is that they can be made with any kind of dry cereal you like. High fiber, unsweetened cereals are the best, but I have to admit I love this recipe made with Corn Pops!

7 cups puffed wheat

1/2 cup each peanuts and dried cranberries (optional)

1/4 cup butter or margarine (non-hydrogenated tub margarine is best)

1 cup packed brown sugar

3 Tbsp cocoa

1/2 cup corn syrup

1 tsp vanilla

1 In a large bowl, stir together puffed wheat, peanuts and cranberries. Combine butter, brown sugar, cocoa and corn syrup in a small saucepan over medium heat. Bring to a boil, stirring often, and cook until smooth.

2 Remove from heat and stir in the vanilla. Pour over the puffed wheat and stir to coat well. Press into an ungreased 9" x 13" pan and refrigerate or leave at room temperature until set. (They are easiest to cut at room temperature.)

Makes 20 squares.

Contents per square

Calories	105
Total fat	2.3 g
saturated fat	0.4 g
monounsaturated fat	0.8 g
polyunsaturated fat	1.1 g
Protein	0.8 g
Carbohydrates	20.8 g
Cholesterol	0.0 mg
Fiber	0.6 g
Calories from fat	20%

Chocolate Fudge

Who doesn't adore fudge? Unfortunately, fudge = pudge. But after much experimentation I came up with a formula for rich chocolate fudge with hardly any fat! Cocoa is a great ingredient to use if you're watching your fat intake – it contains all of the chocolate flavor and virtually none of the fat.

2 cups sugar

1/3 cup cocoa

1/4 tsp salt

2/3 cup 2% milk

2 Tbsp corn syrup

2 Tbsp butter

1 tsp vanilla

1/3 cup chopped walnuts or pecans (optional)

Contents per serving

Calories	167
Total fat	2.2 g
saturated fat	1.4 g
monounsaturated fat	0.7 g
polyunsaturated fat	0.1 g
Protein	0.9 g
Carbohydrates	38.0 g
Cholesterol	5.7 mg
Fiber	1.1 g
Calories from fat	12%

1 Combine the sugar, cocoa, salt, milk and corn syrup in a heavy saucepan set over medium heat. Cook, stirring constantly, until the sugar dissolves. Bring to a boil and cook until the mixture reaches 234 F on a candy thermometer. Remove from heat and add butter and vanilla, but don't stir it – let it sit until it cools to 110 F.

2 Stir vigorously until the mixture loses its gloss (stir in a handful of nuts at this point if you like), and quickly spread into an 8" x 8" pan or a loaf pan that is either non-stick or has been lined with parchment or foil. Cool until set.

Makes 1 pound. Serves about 12.

Sponge Toffee

This was my favorite treat (OK, one of many) when I was a kid. My Mom would buy little blocks of sponge toffee for my sisters and I when she went to the little grocery store by our house, and we'd get chunks of Rundle Rock (the same thing, covered with chocolate) when we went skiing in Banff. It's also known as Sea Foam Candy or Cinder Toffee. True, this doesn't have any nutritional value, but it's fat free and really delicious. When I'm craving something sweet a little chunk of sponge toffee always does the trick for me. Although kids love this stuff, it's not the best recipe to make with them as the sugar mixture gets dangerously hot.

3/4 cup sugar

1/4 cup corn syrup

1 Tbsp baking soda

Contents per serving

Calories	82
Total fat	0.0 g
saturated fat	0.0 g
monounsaturated fat	0.0 g
polyunsaturated fat	0.0 g
Protein	0.0 g
Carbohydrates	21.2 g
Cholesterol	0.0 mg
Fiber	0.0 g
Calories from fat	0%

1. Spray a 9" x 13" pan really well with non-stick spray.

2. Combine the sugar and syrup in a heavy medium saucepan set over medium-low heat. (Make sure there is lots of room in the pan for the mixture to foam up when you stir in the baking soda.) Stir until the sugar begins to melt. Continue to cook, swirling the pan occasionally but not stirring, until the mixture turns a deep caramel color. Watch it carefully – sugar burns fast!

3. Remove from heat and quickly stir in the baking soda. It will foam up like a science experiment! Quickly pour it into the pan and set aside until it has set. To serve, break into chunks.

Serves 10.

Chocolate Nut Brittle

This chocolate brittle is worth compromising your dental work for. It also makes a great gift. If you don't have a candy thermometer, simply pour a thin drizzle of the hot syrup into a glass of ice water – if it is brittle like hard candy and not pliable, it's at the hard-crack stage.

2 cups mixed nuts, such as pecans, almonds and hazelnuts

1¹/2 cups sugar

¹/2 cup corn syrup

¹/3 cup cocoa

¹/2 tsp soda

pinch of salt

Contents per serving

Calories	324
Total fat	14.7 g
saturated fat	1.4 g
monounsaturated fat	10.3 g
polyunsaturated fat	3.0 g
Protein	3.7 g
Carbohydrates	48.3 g
Cholesterol	0.0 mg
Fiber	2.8 g
Calories from fat	40%

Chocolate Popcorn

Pour the hot chocolate mixture over 8 cups of air popped popcorn instead of the nuts, and quickly stir to coat.

1. Preheat oven to 350 F.

2. Spread the nuts on a cookie sheet and toast for 8 - 10 minutes, shaking often, until golden and fragrant. If you are using hazelnuts, rub the toasted nuts in a tea towel to get rid of the skins.

3. Line a cookie sheet with aluminum foil and spray with non-stick spray, or use a silpat baking mat.

4. Combine sugar, corn syrup and 3/4 cup water in a heavy medium-sized saucepan. Cook over medium heat until the sugar dissolves. Increase heat and cook until the mixture reaches 310 F (hard-crack stage) on a candy thermometer. This should take about half an hour. Meanwhile, combine cocoa, baking soda and salt in a small bowl.

5. When the sugar mixture reaches 310 F, remove from heat and stir in the cocoa mixture, then the nuts. Quickly pour the mixture onto the prepared sheet and spread it as thin as possible with a heatproof spatula or the back of a spoon. If you can't get it very thin, wait until it's cooled a bit but still pliable and stretch it more with your fingers.

Cool completely and break into pieces.

Serves about 10.

My Grandma's Peanut Brittle

I framed the old hand-written card with this recipe on it and hung it in my kitchen. Peanut brittle is one of those old-fashioned treats you rarely see anymore, but always get excited about. At least I do! Try crushing peanut brittle and sprinkling it over (or stirring it into) light vanilla ice cream.

1¹/2 cups sugar

¹/2 cup corn syrup

pinch salt

2 cups dry roasted peanuts

1 tsp vanilla

1 tsp baking soda

Contents per serving

Calories	293
Total fat	10.3 g
saturated fat	1.5 g
monounsaturated fat	5.4 g
polyunsaturated fat	3.4 g
Protein	5.2 g
Carbohydrates	47.1 g
Cholesterol	0.0 mg
Fiber	1.9 g
Calories from fat	32%

1 Combine the sugar, corn syrup, salt and 3/4 cup water in a saucepan and bring to a boil over medium-high heat. Stir constantly until the sugar dissolves. Once the sugar has dissolved do not stir, but swirl the pan occasionally until the mixture reaches 325 F (caramel stage) on a candy thermometer.

2 Remove from heat and stir in the peanuts, vanilla and baking soda – the mixture will foam up in the pan. Immediately pour onto a rimmed baking sheet that has been sprayed with non-stick spray and spread out fairly thin with a spatula or the back of a spoon that has been sprayed as well.

3 Cool completely and break into chunks. Store in an airtight container for up to 2 weeks.

Makes about 10 servings.

Hazelnut or Almond Brittle
Replace the peanuts with toasted hazelnuts or sliced almonds.

Quickies

Let's face it; we don't always have time to plan ahead. But there's no need to panic when you have to come up with something delicious in a hurry - with a few quick and easy ideas up your sleeve, you can toss out all those take out menus and stop spending money on packaged snacks. This is real fast food!

If you are what you eat, I'm usually fast, cheap & easy...

Breadsticks

Twist pretzel or pizza dough (see page 92) or thawed frozen bread dough into elegant breadsticks as long or short as you like. Make them fairly thin, place on a cookie sheet and brush with a little egg white or oil, then sprinkle with salt or other seasonings. Bake at 350 F for about 15 minutes, until golden.

Fruit, Nut & Cheese Truffles

Make fruit, nut and cheese truffles by mixing half an 8 oz package of light cream cheese with 1 cup chopped dried fruit, 2 Tbsp orange juice and 1 cup of grated old cheddar or Montery Jack cheese. Roll into balls and roll in toasted sliced almonds to coat.

Crostini with Olive Tapenade

Spread crostini (see page 43) with olive tapenade; top with slices of roasted red pepper and crumbled goat cheese and grind some black pepper over top. Serve as is or run them under the broiler and serve hot.

Sticky Drumsticks

Grill skinless chicken drumsticks, basting with 1/2 cup barbeque sauce spiked with 2 Tbsp curry paste, or with 1/2 cup bottled teriyaki or char siu sauce mixed with 2 crushed cloves of garlic.

Mediterranean Mini Pitas

Spread mini pitas with hummus; sprinkle with chopped roasted red peppers, black olives, torn fresh basil and/or crumbled feta. Bake at 400 F for 5 minutes.

Mini California Pizzas

Spread mini pitas thinly with pesto; top with cooked shrimp, snipped sun-dried tomatoes and crumbled feta. Bake at 400 F for 5 - 7 minutes.

Turkey & Black Bean Tortilla Rolls

Spread flour tortillas with guacamole (see page 60) or mashed avocado and top with thinly sliced roast turkey breast just below the middle. Top turkey with salsa and fresh cilantro and roll up the tortillas tightly. Slice diagonally about 1" thick with a serrated knife.

Phyllo Pizza

Make a thin, elegant pizza crust by layering 6 sheets of phyllo pastry, lightly brushed with olive oil and sprinkled with dry breadcrumbs and grated Parmesan cheese between the layers. Top with cheese and thinly sliced fresh veggies and bake at 350 F for 20 - 30 minutes.

Smoked Salmon Crostini

Stir a small grated purple onion, 1 Tbsp lime juice and 1/2 tsp cumin into a cup of low fat sour cream. Top crostini (see page 43) with thinly sliced smoked salmon, a thin wedge of avocado and a dollop of the flavored sour cream.

Roasted Red Pepper Quesadillas

Sprinkle 4 oz feta or goat cheese, 1 chopped roasted red pepper, and 2 Tbsp chopped black olives between two flour tortillas and grill or cook in a dry sauté pan until golden on both sides and cheese is melted.

Refried Bean Quesadillas

Spread 1/2 cup refried beans or mashed kidney beans, 1/2 cup shredded old cheddar or Monterey Jack cheese, 1 jalapeno pepper, seeded and minced, and 2 Tbsp chopped fresh cilantro between two flour tortillas and grill, or cook in a dry sauté pan until golden on both sides and cheese is melted.

Sticky Peach Chicken Sticks

Stir together 1 cup peach jam, 1/2 cup BBQ sauce, 1 small grated onion and 2 Tbsp soy sauce; marinate bite-sized chunks of chicken breast and thread the pieces on bamboo skewers. Grill or broil until cooked through.

Shrimp with Orange-Chili Hoisin Sauce

Mix 1/4 cup orange juice and 1/2 tsp chili paste into 3/4 cup bottled hoisin sauce; serve with chilled cooked tail-on shrimp for dipping.

Sun-dried Tomato, Pesto, Shrimp & Feta Pizza

Top a pre-baked pizza crust with 1/2 cup basil pesto, 1/3 cup sun-dried tomatoes rehydrated with boiling water and chopped, 1 cup cooked shrimp, peeled and deveined, and about 1/2 cup crumbled feta cheese. Bake at 350 F for 15 - 20 minutes, until golden.

Quick Seafood Dip

Blend half a package of light cream cheese with 1/2 cup cocktail sauce, then stir in a can of cocktail shrimp and a can of crabmeat. Add 1 tsp lemon juice, a pinch of chili powder and a chopped green onion if you have it.

Quick pizza topping ideas:

- 2 cups caramelized onions, 1/4 cup Kalamata olives and 1 cup crumbled feta
- Caramelized onions & garlic with a small amount of cambazola cheese
- Slices of fresh ripe tomato, sliced fresh basil, and mozzarella (Pizza Margherita)
- Roasted vegetables with any kind of cheese you have around
- Caramelized onion cooked with 1 sliced spicy sausage and grated mozzarella
- Potatoes roasted with lemon, rosemary and olive oil, wilted spinach, artichoke hearts and goat cheese or feta
- Roasted Garlic & White Bean Spread (see page 68)
- Garlicky white bean puree, tomatoes and freshly grated Parmesan cheese

Chutney Gingersnaps

Stir together half an 8 oz package of softened light cream cheese, 1/4 cup mango chutney and a pinch of cumin; spread on gingersnaps.

Crunchy Ravioli on a Stick

Boil ravioli or other filled pasta, drain well and roll in dry breadcrumbs and Parmesan cheese to coat. Heat a bit of oil in a nonstick skillet and cook the pasta for a couple minutes per side, until golden. Thread on a bamboo skewer alone or with a meatball, and serve with tomato sauce for dipping.

Jezebel

Stir a tablespoon of Dijon mustard and a couple teaspoons of horseradish into a small jar of apricot or peach preserves, microwave it (you can do it all in the jar) until it's melted, then pour it over a block of light cream cheese. Serve with crackers.

Plum Glazed Chicken

Baste skinless chicken strips with a mixture of 3 Tbsp soy sauce, 3 Tbsp honey, 2 Tbsp plum sauce and 1 tsp Five spice powder. Thread onto a bamboo skewer and grill or broil until cooked through.

Curried Shrimp Salad Cups

Toss 1/2 lb of cooked shrimp with 1/4 cup light mayonnaise, 2 Tbsp chopped fresh cilantro, 1 Tbsp mango chutney, a good squeeze of lime juice and 1/2 tsp Thai green curry paste. Use it to fill baked wonton cups (see page 122) and garnish with extra cilantro leaves.

Stuffed Mushrooms

Use thick spreads or tart fillings to stuff mushroom caps if you have the gumption to stuff mushrooms! Some say life is too short to stuff a mushroom. I'm a fan of them so I think they're worth the effort. Sprinkle with breadcrumbs and a little Parmesan before you bake them at 350 F until bubbly.

Sticky Balsamic Prosciutto-Wrapped Dates

Bring 1/2 cup each balsamic vinegar and water and 1/4 cup sugar to a simmer in a saucepan set over medium heat. Add 24 whole pitted dates and simmer for 10 minutes. Wrap each date in a thin slice of prosciutto; place on a baking sheet and brush with any remaining balsamic syrup. Bake at 350 F for 5 - 10 minutes. These are like candy!

Stuffed Pretzel Nuggets

Split store-bought or homemade pretzel nuggets (see page 29) in half and spread with a mixture of 2 Tbsp peanut butter and 2 Tbsp salsa, or with any of the schmears on page 81.

Pizza Rolls

Spread flour tortillas with pizza sauce and sprinkle with chopped sautéed onions and peppers and some grated cheese. Roll them up and bake seam-side-down on a cookie sheet at 400 F for about 10 minutes, until the cheese melts. Slice each roll into four pieces and serve warm. (These are great to make in advance and freeze – just pop frozen pizza rolls in the oven for an instant after-school snack.)

Peach-Cambozola Bundles

Wrap thinly sliced prosciutto around a ripe peach wedge and a thin slice of Cambozola.

Thai Chicken Rolls

Spread flour tortillas with a mixture of 2 Tbsp each peanut butter, light mayonnaise and lime juice, 1 clove of crushed garlic and 1 tsp grated ginger. Top with slices of roasted chicken breast, slivered red pepper and a handful of torn fresh basil; roll them up, tucking in the ends like a burrito, and cut in half diagonally.

Easy Chicken or Beef Satay

Mix 1/4 cup each BBQ sauce, peanut butter and soy sauce and use it to marinate a pound of chicken or beef strips. Thread onto soaked bamboo skewers and grill for 5 - 7 minutes, until cooked through. Simmer any remaining marinade in a small saucepan or in the microwave and serve alongside for dipping.

Strawberry Cheesecake Bites

Hollow out large strawberries and fill them with low fat cream cheese sweetened with some icing sugar and a drop of vanilla. Top with a couple of sliced almonds. They're like a mouthful of cheesecake!

Chili Cheese Fries

Top oven baked fries (see page 10) with warmed chili (homemade or Stagg's vegetarian chili, which is very low in fat and full of nutritious legumes) and a grating of old cheddar cheese. Make sure the chili is hot so that the cheese melts onto it!

Salami Chips

Lay thin slices of pepper salami (or your favorite kind) in a single layer on a baking sheet; cover with parchment, then another layer of salami if you like. Bake at 350 F for 15 - 20 minutes, until crispy and most of the fat has been rendered. Blot with a paper towel. Peel from the parchment and serve warm.

Tortilla Cups

Cut rounds out of flour tortillas with a small cookie cutter. Brush with a bit of oil and press into mini muffin cups; bake at 350 F for about 10 minutes, until golden. Fill with any filling you like – the Chorizo Chipotle Dip (see page 58) and Creamy Chicken & Charred Corn Dip (see page 59) are especially good!

Peanut Butter Popcorn Balls

Melt a bag of marshmallows with 1/2 cup light peanut butter in the microwave and use it to coat 8 cups of air popped popcorn. Shape into popcorn balls while the mixture is still warm.

Granola Bites

Stir together 2 cups low fat granola (see page 18), 1/4 cup peanut butter, 2 Tbsp honey and a few tablespoons of milk – as much as you need to hold the mixture together. Roll into bite-sized balls and chill until firm.

Stuffed Apricots

Stuff plump dried apricots with a mixture of equal parts blue cheese and light cream cheese.

Olive Deviled Eggs

Make deviled eggs by replacing half the yolks with heart-healthy Olive Tapenade (see page 74); sprinkle with chopped flat-leaf parsley.

Real Fruit Gummies

Puree 2 lbs of dried fruit (any kind or a combination) in a food processor with just enough hot water to make it very smooth. Spread about 1/4" thick on a rimmed non-stick cookie sheet and bake at 200 F for several hours, or at 150 F overnight, until the fruit is soft but firm with a gummy texture. Let it cool and cut into squares or little shapes with a small cookie cutter.

Spicy Garlic Nuts

Sauté 2 crushed cloves of garlic in 1 Tbsp olive oil for a minute, and then stir in 2/3 cup each almonds, peanuts and cashews. Add 2 tsp Worcestershire and 1 tsp each cayenne pepper and chili powder and cook for a few minutes. Cool and toss with a cup of pretzel sticks and a teaspoon of sea salt.

Quick Veggie Dip

If you have some plain yogurt or low fat sour cream in the fridge, add a few spoonfuls of light mayo and some chopped fresh herbs, curry paste, pesto, chutney, sweet chili sauce or roasted garlic for a quick veggie dip.

Creamy Avocado Ranch Dip

Stir 1 mashed avocado with 1 package of Ranch salad dressing mix (or any other kind), 1 cup of low fat sour cream, 1 chopped tomato and 1 Tbsp lemon juice. Serve with tortilla chips.

Tofu Peanut Dip

Whiz together 1/2 cup each light peanut butter and silken tofu, 3 Tbsp brown sugar, 2 Tbsp each lime juice and soy sauce, 2 crushed cloves of garlic and a few drops Tabasco for a creamy peanut dip with the nutritional benefits of soy.

Easy Bean Dip

Combine 1 can kidney beans, rinsed and drained, 1 large clove of crushed garlic, 1 Tbsp lime juice and 1/2 tsp each chili powder and cumin in a food processor and pulse until as chunky or smooth as you like it.

Prosciutto Prawns

Wrap uncooked tail-on prawns with a thin piece of prosciutto and grill for 3 - 4 minutes, until pink. These are fantastic dipped in pesto!

Chutney Cream Cheese Schmear

Mix 8 oz tub of light cream cheese with 1/4 cup peach or mango chutney and 1/4 cup chopped dried cranberries. This is also good with apricot jam and chopped dried apricots.

Roasted Feta with Red Peppers and Olives

Roast 1/2" slices of good feta cheese in a shallow dish under the broiler until golden and bubbly around the edges. Sprinkle with a little oregano and fresh pepper and top with a chopped roasted red pepper, a handful of Kalamata olives and a drizzle of olive oil. Serve with pita chips.

Caramel Apples

Make rich caramel apples with only 3 grams of fat by melting 25 caramels with 2 Tbsp water over medium-low heat until smooth. Push Popsicle sticks into 6 apples and dip them in the warm caramel to coat. Place upright on a cookie sheet or in paper muffin liners and chill until set.

Honey Roasted Onion & Garlic Dip

Roast 2 chopped onions and head of peeled garlic with a tablespoon of olive oil and honey; pulse in a food processor until chunky with 1/2 cup light sour cream, salt and pepper. Serve with crackers or potato chips.

Mexican Wonton Packets

Put spoonfuls of Bean Dip (see page 186) or Chorizo Chipotle Dip (see page 58) into the middle of wonton wrappers, moisten the edges, fold in half and press to seal. Brush them with a bit of oil and bake at 400 F for 6 - 8 minutes, until golden. Serve with guacamole (see page 60) or salsa.

Real Fruit Leather

Puree a few peeled fresh peaches, nectarines or apricots in a food processor until very smooth. Spread it as thin and evenly as you can on a rimmed non-stick cookie sheet, or a sheet lined with parchment or a silpat baking mat. Bake at 200 F for 3 - 4 hours, until dry and leathery but still slightly tacky. Peel the leather off the pan, cut it into pieces or strips, roll it up and store in a zip-lock bag.

Ginger Molasses Ice Cream Sandwiches

Freeze Ginger Molasses Crinkles (see page 162) and spread with softened light ice cream. Sandwich with another cookie and roll the edge in chopped toasted almonds, if you like.

Mud Pie Ice Cream Sandwiches

Spread about 2 Tbsp softened light ice cream onto purchased chocolate wafer cookies (or use the recipe on page 164), drizzling with a little Hershey's chocolate syrup or butterscotch syrup and topping with a second cookie. Freeze until firm and roll the edges in finely chopped nuts if you like.

Lettuce Wraps with Figs, Roasted Red Peppers and Parmesan

Arrange a wedge of iceberg or the small inner leaves of Romaine lettuce on a platter with some sliced fresh or dried figs, sliced roasted red peppers and fresh Parmesan shavings. Put a little of each in a lettuce leaf, roll it up and eat. (This is my Mom's favorite appetizer!)

Smoothies

Smoothies make an awesome snack or meal in a glass. Whiz 1 cup of yogurt, a banana, 2 cups fresh or frozen berries, 1/4 cup milk, 1 - 2 Tbsp honey and 1 cup ice in a blender until smooth. For added protein, add some tofu.

Olive & Feta Salsa

Stir together a chopped ripe tomato and 1/4 cup each: chopped cucumber, purple onion, Kalamata olives and feta cheese. Add some cilantro if you have it. This is great stuffed into mini pitas with hummus!

Chocolate Panini

Place a slice of good-quality bread (you don't need to butter it) in a skillet set over medium heat, and sprinkle with chopped or grated dark chocolate. Top with another slice and cook, pressing down with the back of a spatula, until the bread is golden and the chocolate begins to melt. Carefully turn over and cook for a few more minutes, until it's golden on both sides.

Roasted Pumpkin Seeds

Toss 2 cups of washed and dried pumpkin seeds with 1 Tbsp canola oil, 1 tsp salt and 1/2 tsp each cayenne, curry powder or chili powder and cumin. Roast at 350 F for 45 minutes, until crisp and golden.

Index

Cheese Sticks 88
Cheesecake Muffins 149
Cheesy Black Bean Dip 57
Chili Cheese Fries 185
Chili con Queso Dip 55
Chorizo Chipotle Dip 58
Chutney Cream Cheese Schmear 186
Chutney Gingersnaps 183
Crab, Spinach & Artichoke Dip 52
Cranberry Orange Goat Cheese Schmear 81
Creamy & Spicy Tuna Schmear 81
Creamy Chicken & Charred Corn Dip 59
Curried Shrimp Chutney Dip 67
Feta Chili Dip 73
Focaccia 170
Fruit, Nut & Cheese Truffles 182
Hot Crab & Artichoke Dip 53
Jalapeno Poppers 134
Jezebel 183
Mini California Pizzas 182
Mushroom & Onion Stromboli 132
Olive & Feta Focaccia 171
Olive & Feta Salsa 187
Parmesan Toasts 43
Parmesan, Olive & Sun-dried
   Tomato Biscuits 166
Peach-Cambozola Bundles 184
Phyllo Pizza 182
Pizza Pretzels 29
Pizza Rolls 184
Potato Skins 95
Quick Seafood Dip 183
Refried Bean Quesadillas 183
Roasted Feta with Red Peppers and Olives 186
Roasted Red Pepper & Feta Dip 73
Roasted Red Pepper Quesadillas 182
Salsa Poppers 134
Salsa Spinach & Artichoke Dip 52
Sesame Parmesan Crackers 37
Sesame, Garlic & Parmesan Wonton Crisps 44
Seven Layer Dip 56
Spanakopita (Spinach & Feta) Triangles 128
Spicy Cheese Fries 11
Spinach & Artichoke Dip 52
Spinach con Queso Dip 55
Strawberry Cheesecake Bites 185
Stromboli 132
Stuffed Apricots 185
Stuffed Mushrooms 184
Stuffed Pizza Bites with Saucy Dip 133
Sun Dried Tomato & Parmesan Biscotti 159

Sun-dried Tomato, Pesto,
   Shrimp and Feta Pizza 183
Three Cheese Caramelized Onion,
   Spinach & Mushroom Calzone 131
Tuna Stuffed Tomatoes 135
Warm Chevre Dip 54
White Bean, Tomato & Olive Bruschetta
   with Goat Cheese 101
Yogurt & Feta White Bean Spread 69
Cheese Bagels 169
Cheese Biscuits 166
Cheese Sticks 88
Cheesecake Muffins 149
Cheesy Black Bean Dip 57
Chewy Honey Energy Bars 30
Chicken:
   BBQ Buffalo Chicken Strips
      with Blue Cheese Dip 113
   BBQ Chicken Pizza 93
   Chicken Fingers with Honey Mustard Dip 84
   Chicken Negimaki 138
   Chicken Satay with Peanut Sauce 108
   Chicken, Black Bean
      & Mushroom Quesadillas 102
   Chicken, Spinach, Sun-dried Tomato
      & Feta Triangles 129
   Creamy Chicken & Charred Corn Dip 59
   Crispy Sesame Chicken Fingers 85
   Crunchy Buffalo Chicken Fingers 85
   Curried Almond Chicken Fingers 84
   Curried Chicken Phyllo Triangles 129
   Curried Chicken Salad Mini Pita Pockets 126
   Curried Coconut Mango Chicken
      in Wonton Cups 122
   Easy Chicken or Beef Satay 184
   Hoisin Chicken Lettuce Wraps 130
   Honey, Garlic & Ginger Sesame
      Chicken Sticks 116
   Jerk Chicken Skewers 112
   Pecan Crusted Chicken Fingers 84
   Plum Glazed Chicken 184
   Spicy Chicken Fingers 85
   Sticky Drumsticks 182
   Sticky Peach Chicken Sticks 183
   Sticky, Spicy Drumsticks 87
   Tandoori Chicken Satay 111
   Thai Chicken Rolls 184
Chicken Fingers with Honey Mustard Dip 84
Chicken Negimaki 138
Chicken Satay with Peanut Sauce 108
Chicken, Black Bean & Mushroom

Creamy Avocado Ranch Dip 186
Creamy Baba Ghanouj 71
Creamy Chicken & Charred Corn Dip 59
Creamy Fruit Dip 80
Creamy Key Lime Dip 80
Curried Shrimp Chutney Dip 67
Curried Veggie Dip 77
Dulce de Leche 80
Edamamole 61
Feta Chili Dip 73
Fresh Pea Hummus 67
Fruit Dips 80
Guacamole 60
Guacamole with Pears,
   Grapes & Pomegranate 60
Hot Crab & Artichoke Dip 53
Hummus 66
Italian White Bean Spread 69
Marshmallow Peach Fruit Dip 80
Mediterranean Hummus 67
Muhammara 79
Mushroom Tapenade 74
Olive & Basil Salsa 63
Olive & Sun Dried Tomato Tapenade 74
Olive Tapenade 74
Peanut Sauce 109
Pico de Gallo 64
Pumpkin Hummus 67
Radish & Roasted Red Pepper Dip 76
Roasted Carrot Hummus 67
Roasted Eggplant & Tomato Dip 71
Roasted Garlic & White Bean Spread 68
Roasted Garlic Edamame Hummus 67
Roasted Garlic Hummus 67
Roasted Red Pepper & Feta Dip 73
Roasted Red Pepper & Garlic Dip 72
Roasted Red Pepper Hummus 67
Romesco Dip 78
Salsa Spinach & Artichoke Dip 52
Seven Layer Dip 56
Spicy Hummus 67
Spinach & Artichoke Dip 52
Spinach con Queso Dip 55
Strawberry Fruit Dip 80
Sweet Red Pepper Dip 139
Tofu Peanut Dip 186
Tzatziki 70
Warm Chevre Dip 54
White Bean & Roasted Red Pepper Spread 69
White Bean Guacamole 69
Yogurt & Feta White Bean Spread 69

Dip, Spread, Dunk & Smear 51
Dried Fruit & Nut Scones 143
Dulce de Leche 80

Easy Bean Dip 186
Easy Chicken or Beef Satay 184
Edamamole 61

Feta Chili Dip 73
Finger Lickin' Food 83
Five Spice Almonds 26
Flavored Popcorn 15
Flax Wheat Thins 40
Flaxseed Wafers 37
Flour Tortillas 45
Focaccia 170
Food on a Stick 107
Fresh Pea Hummus 67
Fruit & Nut Soda Bread 148
Fruit Dips 80
Fruit, Nut & Cheese Truffles 182

Garlic Dipping Sauce 127
Garlic Peanuts 29
Garlic Pepper Pecans 22
Garlic Roasted Potato Skins 41
Garlicky Scallop Potstickers 136
Ginger Mango Dipping Sauce 127
Ginger Molasses Crinkle Sandwiches 162
Ginger Molasses Crinkles 162
Ginger Molasses Ice Cream Sandwiches 187
Good Things in Small Packages 121
Goong Waan 90
Got the Munchies? 9
Granola 18
Granola Bites 185
Granola to Go 18
Grape Focaccia 171
Greek Lamb Kebabs 114
Greek Meatballs 114
Greek Mini Pita Pockets 125
Green Eggs with Ham 96
Guacamole 60
Guacamole with Pears, Grapes
   & Pomegranate 60

Hazelnut or Almond Brittle 179
Hoisin Chicken Lettuce Wraps 130
Honey Roasted Almonds 26
Honey Roasted Nut & Seed Clusters 27
Honey Roasted Onion & Garlic Dip 186

Honey Roasted Peppered Almonds & Pecans 26
Honey, Garlic & Ginger Sesame
  Chicken Sticks 116
Honey, Ginger & Sesame Salmon Sticks 116
Honey-Mustard Salmon Sticks 116
Hot Crab & Artichoke Dip 53
Hot Soft Pretzels 28
Hummus 66

Irish Soda Bread 48
Italian White Bean Spread 69

Jalapeno Poppers 134
Jelly Fauxnuts 149
Jerk Chicken Skewers 112
Jezebel 183

Kettle Corn 13

Lamb Kabobs, Greek 114
Lemon Banana Bread 144
Lemon Poppyseed Crackers 36
Lettuce Wraps with Figs,
  Roasted Red Peppers & Parmesan 187
Lovin' from the Oven 141

Maple Cinnamon Pecans 22
Maple Cranberry Pecan Popcorn 14
Maple Pecan Popcorn 14
Marshmallow Peach Fruit Dip 80
Mediterranean Hummus 67
Mediterranean Mini Pitas 182
Meringue Nuts 24
Mexican Wonton Pockets 186
Mini California Pizzas 182
Mini Flour Tortillas 45
Mini Toad-in-the-Hole 89
Mini Yorkshire Puddings with Roast Beef &
Horseradish Cream 89
Mud Pie Ice Cream Sandwiches 187
Muffins & Quickbreads:
  Apple Muesli Bread 145
  Apple Muesli Muffins 145
  Banana Bread 144
  Banana Muffins 144
  Cheesecake Muffins 149
  Chocolate Swirl Banana Bread 144
  Cranberry Pumpkin Pecan Bread 147
  Cranberry Pumpkin Pecan Muffins 147
  Crumb Cakes 149
  Jelly Fauxnuts 149

  Lemon Banana Bread 144
  Whole Wheat Berry Bread 145
  Whole Wheat Nut Bread 145
  Zucchini Lemon Walnut Bread 146
  Zucchini Lemon Walnut Muffins 146
Muhammara 79
Mushroom & Onion Stromboli 132
Mushroom Tapenade 74
My Grandma's Peanut Brittle 179
My Granola 18

Nuoc Cham 127
Nut(s):
  Chili Honey Roasted Almonds 26
  Five Spice Almonds 26
  Garlic Peanuts 29
  Garlic Pepper Pecans 22
  Honey Roasted Almonds 26
  Honey Roasted Nut & Seed Clusters 27
  Honey Roasted Peppered Almonds
    & Pecans 26
  Maple Cinnamon Pecans 22
  Maple Pecan Popcorn 14
  Meringue Nuts 24
  Spiced Maple Pecans 22
  Spiced Meringue Nuts 24
  Sue's Spiced Nuts 23
  Sweet Spiced Pecans 25

Olive & Basil Salsa 63
Olive & Feta Focaccia 171
Olive & Feta Salsa 187
Olive & Garlic Breadsticks 182
Olive & Garlic Pretzels 28
Olive & Sun Dried Tomato Tapenade 74
Olive Devilled Eggs 185
Olive Oil & Garlic Bagel Chips 43
Olive Tapenade 74
One Bite Brownies 155
Onion & Garlic Bagels 169
Onion Bialys 169
Oven Fries 10

Parmesan Toasts 43
Parmesan, Olive & Sun-dried Tomato
  Biscuits 166
Party Mix 16
Peach-Cambozola Bundles 184
Peach Crumble Cake 153
Peanut Brittle, My Grandma's 179
Peanut Butter & Honey Gorp 31

Sponge Toffee 177
Sticky Balsamic Prosciutto-Wrapped Dates 184
Sticky Drumsticks 182
Sticky Peach Chicken Sticks 183
Sticky, Spicy Drumsticks 87
Stone Fruit Tarts 174
Strawberry Cheesecake Bites 185
Strawberry Fruit Dip 80
Stromboli 132
Stuffed Apricots 185
Stuffed Mushrooms 184
Stuffed Pizza Bites with Saucy Dip 133
Stuffed Pretzel Nuggets 184
Sue's Spiced Nuts 23
Sun Dried Tomato & Parmesan Biscotti 159
Sun-dried Tomato, Pesto, Shrimp
   and Feta Pizza 183
Sweet & Spicy Sweet Potato Fries 11
Sweet Eats 173
Sweet Hoisin Meatballs 119
Sweet Lime Dipping Sauce 127
Sweet Potato Oven Fries 10
Sweet Red Pepper Dip 139
Sweet Spiced Pecans 25

Tandoori Chicken Satay 111
Teriyaki Beef Sticks 115
Thai Chicken Rolls 184
Three Cheese Caramelized Onion,
   Spinach & Mushroom Calzone 131
Tofu Peanut Dip 186
Tomato Basil Wheat Thins 40
Tomato, Avocado & Shrimp Bruschetta 102
Tortilla Chips, Baked 46
Tortilla Chips, Cinnamon Sugar 46
Tortilla Cups 185
Trail Mix 19
Tuna Stuffed Tomatoes 135
Turkey & Black Bean Tortilla Rolls 182
Tzatziki 70

Vietnamese Pork Meatballs 117
Vietnamese Rice Paper Rolls 127

Warm Chevre Dip 54
Wheat Thins 40
White Bean & Roasted Red Pepper Spread 69
White Bean Guacamole 69
White Bean, Tomato & Olive Bruschetta
   with Goat Cheese 101
Whole Wheat Banana Walnut Scones 143

Whole Wheat Berry Bread 145
Whole Wheat Nut Bread 145
Wonton Crisps 44
World's Best Peanut Butter Cookies 159
Yogurt & Feta White Bean Spread 69
Yogurt Mint Sauce 114

Zucchini Lemon Walnut Bread 146
Zucchini Lemon Walnut Muffins 146